Creating Worlds, Constructing Meaning

Creating Worlds, Constructing Meaning

The Scottish Storyline® Method

Jeff Creswell

Foreword by Bobbi Fisher

HEINEMANN
Portsmouth, NH

Heinemann

361 Hanover Street
Portsmouth, NH 03801–3912

Offices and agents throughout the world

Acknowledgments for borrowed material can be found on p. 124.

Library of Congress Cataloging-in-Publication Data

Creswell, Jeff.
Creating worlds, constructing meaning : the Scottish storyline method / Jeff Creswell ; foreword by Bobbi Fisher.
p. cm.
ISBN 0-435-07244-7
1. Active learning. 2. Group work in education. 3. Project method in teaching. 4. Storytelling. 5. Interdisciplinary approach in education. 6. Education, Elementary—Activity programs.
I. Title.
LB1027.23.C74 1997
371.39—dc21 97-30219
CIP

Editor: William Varner
Production: Vicki Kasabian
Cover design: Mary Parker
Manufacturing: Louise Richardson

Printed in the United States of America on acid-free paper
T&C Digital

To Kathy
(1952–1994)

Contents

Foreword

Bobbi Fisher

The children in Jeff Creswell's classroom introduced me to Scottish Storyline during my visit to their school in February 1996. This group of fourth and fifth graders had recently finished the Huk-Toocht Fish Farm Storyline and were beginning to develop characters and create the setting for the Underground to Canada Storyline.

The children knew I was coming and welcomed me warmly as I entered the room. First, I sat in on a class meeting, during which the students described their newly created characters and discussed some of the people and incidents they might encounter along the Underground Railroad as the topic developed. Next, one of the children showed me her topic book with all the pertinent work she had for the Huk-Toocht Fish Farm. For the remainder of the morning, I conversed with different children as they worked on the maps in their Underground Railroad journals, figuring out the distance between two stops on the journey by measuring on a map and using the scale. They all exhibited great pride in their work and enthusiastically answered my questions. It was clear to me that they wanted to be sure that I understood all about Storyline.

I was struck by the learning and caring that pervaded everything the children did: they were extremely engaged in their work; the scholarship was rigorous; and they were building community as they pursued a common topic. Children of diverse backgrounds, talents, and learning abilities were working together and helping and sharing with each other because they were all intensely interested in what they were learning.

Where was Jeff while the children were teaching me? He was teaching—talking with children about their characters, helping them define what they wanted to say, matching children to solve common problems, and celebrating discoveries. He was also learning—listening to what the children had discovered, hearing their stories, reading new material, and planning new directions that the Storyline might take.

It was very apparent that Jeff's expertise as a teacher provided the support for this community of engaged learners. His attitude was a catalyst for the positive learning environment. His enthusiasm for Storyline, coupled with his genuine trust in all of his students as learners, gave them confidence in their ability to introduce me to the method.

As I left the school that day, I was convinced that the Storyline method provides an authentic curriculum framework in which all students, regardless of the grade, become engaged in rigorous learning in a caring environment. Open *Creating Worlds, Constructing Meaning* and let the students teach you about Storyline.

Acknowledgments

First and foremost I must thank Steve Bell and Sallie Harkness. As two of the originators of the Scottish Storyline Method, they have travelled all over the world sharing this wonderful idea. It was their willingness to come to the West Coast that first brought Storyline to the United States. They have been my inspiration from the beginning.

This book has been influenced by many people. It is the tip of an iceberg. Many have helped to shape me as a teacher and a writer. It has been my privilege to work with so many exceptional people.

Many thanks to Colin Dunkeld, my first true mentor; to Lindy Delf, Tony Wolk, and Shelly Reese for helping me to see that I was a writer; to Donna Strom, Jan Zuckerman, Lisa Parks, and Rebecca Plaskitt for teaching me about the joys of team teaching; to my principal, Pam Shelly, who has encouraged and supported me in developing the Storyline method in my classroom over the last ten years.

Eileen Vopelak is my Storyline partner in California. I couldn't have done this book without her support and editorial advice. The book is stronger because of her expertise. Shelly Othus is the office manager for Storyline Design, and her skill at running a small consulting business enabled me to continue to teach full-time and write this book. She is the business person I am not, and I am grateful for her willingness to share her talents so we can present the Storyline method to teachers through our classes.

I acknowledge the power of people like Donald Graves, Lucy Calkins, Nancie Atwell, Mary Ellen Giacobbe, Peter Elbow, Bobbi Fisher, and Regie Routman, who have inspired me by their willingness to open up their teaching to me. I have used their ideas, not as recipes, but rather as menus, giving me things to try with my own children in my own unique learning environment.

Carolyn Coman, formerly of Heinemann, followed her curiosity and came to a workshop on "The Scottish Storyline Method" because she had never seen the word "Scottish" in the title of a presentation at an educational conference. She had the belief that the Storyline method could be shared in a book and the vision of what that book could be. Her positive nurturing gave me the confidence to keep writing. Bill Varner stepped in when Carolyn retired to write full time, and he carried on by encouraging and sharpening the vision.

Finally, I want to thank my family. My wife Sarah has encouraged me through every step of the process. She has listened to my ideas, tried many in her own classroom, and has given me the freedom to hole up and write! My three children, Jennifer, Joel, and Katherine, put up with a Dad who was often preoccupied and frequently distracted. They kept me honest and helped me to have a life outside of my work. I am blessed to have such a caring group of people around me.

Prologue

The Storyline Method: How It All Began

Sallie Coverly Harkness

The approach now known as the "Storyline" method was developed by a small group of educators based in the inservice department of Jordanhill College of Education in Glasgow. At that time I was working closely with colleagues Steve Bell and Fred Rendell. Our names are associated with the Storyline initiative, but it was developed empirically as a result of our collaboration with classroom teachers, partly in response to problems and difficulties they identified, and partly in response to an important report published by the Scottish Office Education Department in 1965.

This document, which was to provide guidelines for Scottish teachers for the next twenty-five years, put children—their growth and development—first, taking into account home, school, and neighborhood, and saw the education service as working alongside health and social services. The following quotations will give you some insight into the philosophy:

> The pattern of education in the primary years must have regard for the nature of the child and for the way he grows and develops during this period.

> The most fundamental changes are those which have arisen from the growing acceptance by teachers of the principles underlying an education based on the needs and interests of the child and the nature of the world in which he is growing up. Through a wide range of experiences the pupil is given opportunities to participate actively in his own learning. As a result, his approach to what is to be learned is livelier and his final understanding deeper. In addition, his whole attitude to work may be so improved that he is anxious to continue learning.

> It cannot be too strongly stressed that education is concerned as much with the personal development of the child as with the teaching of

> subjects. How the child learns is educationally no less important than what he learns. Certainly, skills must be mastered, knowledge must be acquired, and the curriculum must be carefully planned to ensure that basic skills and essential knowledge are adequately covered. Primary education, however, will have failed the age and society it serves if children leave the primary school without the right attitude to learning, or the resource and will to continue and further their own education.

Views of the curriculum were changing too:

> The curriculum is not to be thought of as a number of discrete subjects, each requiring a specific allocation of time each week or each month. Indeed, it is quite impossible to treat the subjects of the curriculum in isolation from one another if education is to be meaningful to the child. The chapters that follow describe many ways in which the curriculum can be organized so as to effect linkage between subjects. Many of the activities that are recommended involve elements of more than one "subject," and serve to advance the pupils' knowledge and skill in more than one field. Thus linguistic and mathematical skills find application in environmental studies; art and craft activities, drama and music play a part in history and geography; projects and centers of interest embrace many different branches of the curriculum. "Integration" of this kind should be a feature of primary education at all stages.

In many schools these recommendations created the need for a radical change of approach. Hitherto teachers had based their curriculum on the use of textbook series for the different subjects. Pupils recorded their progress by moving from page to page and chapter to chapter. When these outdated texts were removed, some teachers did not know what to put in their place. In this respect the '65 memorandum (Primary Education in Scotland) did not provide much practical help. The document was strong on principle but weak on practical advice.

In the late sixties and seventies, we were fortunate that funding was available for curriculum development and inservice. Local authority education departments were setting up advisory services to support in-school developments. Mainly due to the efforts of our far-sighted boss, John Angus Smith, then Vice Principal of Jordanhill, members of the staff tutor group were freed from work with preservice students to help class teachers develop their practice in order to meet the requirements of the memorandum. The main objectives were to introduce child-centered approaches, active and discovery learning, integration of the curriculum, and to encourage differentiated groupwork.

In order to achieve these objectives we had to find a context in which we could introduce these ideas. We also had to find ways of showing teachers how the ideas could work in practice. After some preliminary experimentation and development work in schools a new kind of inservice course began to emerge. This took the form of a three-day workshop for class teachers. A topic was selected and a Storyline and activities designed to develop it. When teachers came to the course they were asked to take part in the Storyline activities, putting themselves in the place of the pupils.

During these workshops the group itself, usually about twenty teachers, was a powerful tool in learning. As they worked through Storyline episodes teachers became imaginatively involved in answering key questions, solving problems, and speculating. Characters were invented, incidents suggested and explored. Very simple materials and techniques were used to create artwork that recorded and illustrated ideas and feelings. In a natural way teachers learned how groupwork could be organized and how many aspects of the curriculum could be integrated into one topic. They also learned of the vital importance of ordering the topic into a series of logical steps.

Many different Storyline topics were generated and shared. These showed how the approach could be adapted to suit children of all ages and abilities, and that the balance of the curriculum focus could be flexible: some topics had a high content of history, geography, or health. All Storylines were seen as vehicles for developing language skills, and in the case of book-based topics, a high literary content could be achieved. Book-based topics proved to be very popular with Scottish teachers, who welcomed the security that working from a book can bring.

The development of the Storyline approach took place over a long period of time. The workshop courses started around 1970 proved to be very popular and were continued for many years. The school-based experiment and consultation also continued. As the years passed by, teachers who had been involved in classroom practice were promoted to Head Teachers (principals). They introduced the Storyline approach to their staff, and through the school programs developed the method to provide for continuity and progression. While this process was ongoing, the Staff Tutor Team refined, developed, and published material, and as new members joined the group the scope of the work was extended and new ideas were integrated into the Storyline framework. In the eighties the fame of the Storyline method began to spread, and members of the Staff Tutor Team were invited to run workshops in other countries. Visitors from abroad began to come to Glasgow to see how Storyline topics were used in Scottish schools.

The Storyline approach—with its simple framework of Storyline, key questions, and activities—has stood the test of time and the increasing weight of an expanding curriculum. Its flexibility has permitted teachers and curriculum developers to adapt it to their own purposes. It has traveled well and proved its worth in various cultures and educational systems. Thirty years on, it is very well established in the west of Scotland, where it is so much a part of accepted classroom practice that it is seldom identified by name as a particular methodological approach. It is very encouraging to know that Storyline is proving itself in the United States. I have every reason to believe that it will flourish there, giving challenge to students and job satisfaction to their teachers.

It's wonderful to feel that I have been part of this worldwide development, but I think that the success of the Storyline approach lies more in what it is, rather than who is promoting it. Over the years it has been possible to identify some of the key features of a successful Storyline.

First of all, it encourages a creative partnership between teacher and learners, in which ideas and feelings are shared, explored, and built upon. Although the teacher may be in control of the structure and direction of the topic and should have identified the desired learning that pupils will undertake within it, the Storyline topic may only be developed as a result of the contributions and responses of the learners. As a matter of principle, all Storylines start from what pupils already know and acknowledge in their previous learning. However, as they suggest answers, provide solutions to problems, and create characters and scenarios, their involvement and commitment is increased, and they feel ownership of the Storyline and the learning they are achieving within it. This sense of ownership and the degree of imaginative involvement is one aspect which marks the Storyline approach as different from other topic work or projects. Also significant is that pupils are asked to create their own mental models *before* looking at reality. Having explored and expressed ideas in the classroom before going on a visit or receiving a visitor, pupils are alerted to key issues. Their questions have a focus and they bring knowledge to the situation.

All over the world teachers who adopt the Storyline approach have found that their pupils are motivated to learn; pupil/teacher and pupil/pupil relationships are improved; groupwork has a sense of purpose; different aspects of the curriculum can be integrated; activity methods can be managed, discovery learning guided, and resources well used; parents become interested and involved; opportunities to forge links with the community can be developed; cooperative teaching is possible; planning and preparation can be structured; pupils can express and record their ideas through a variety of media; pupil output enhances a sense of achievement and builds confidence; skills are practiced in relevant and meaningful contexts; and everyone can have fun and enjoyment learning in this way. The most regular comment from pupils is that Storyline is "better than work."

Now read on and enjoy Jeff Creswell's personal account of his own Storyline journey, but after that you'd best sign on for a Storyline workshop because if you really want to know about the Storyline method you have to experience it yourself.

1 *My Own Beginnings*

The first time I met Kathy Fifield was in the fall of 1981. I was assigned to do a field experience in her kindergarten classroom. I arrived early on a sunny autumn morning to the ugly army-green cement-block building that was the Sumner Elementary School. It would have surprised me less if it had said "State Penitentiary" on the sign. Kathy was not yet there when I arrived, so I awkwardly sat down in the teachers' lounge to wait. I actually heard Kathy before I ever saw her. The echo of her laughter down the hall preceded her by a good thirty seconds, long enough for me to wonder who was the blazing extrovert making all the noise. When she came into view around the corner—fur coat, bright red lipstick, dangly earrings, and arms full of a jumble of books—I knew instinctively that she was the person I was going to work with.

I followed her through the corridors and out to her double classroom like a lost puppy, hoping that I had at last found a home. By the end of three months in her classroom we had become fast friends, and I was invited to student teach with her that spring. I didn't realize then that sixteen years later Kathy would still have a profound effect on the way I teach.

My first teaching job was in inner-city Portland, teaching fourth and fifth grade to lower-income African American children. The Humboldt School was in a pretty rough part of town. I was petrified. Although I had worked as an assistant at a similar school for four years, all of my experience was in early childhood, below third grade.

I was given a classroom originally intended for first grade and left to my own devices. I can remember driving through Portland and checking out school boiler rooms to find excess furniture, as my classroom had only first-grade furniture and supplies. I didn't receive any teacher's manuals or student texts until January of that first year. I remember my routine of teaching all day, bringing everything home that night, and spending the evening planning the next day. I designed my own program because I had no choice. By the time I did receive the textbooks I was pretty happy with most of what I was doing, so I began to look for models of more holistic ways of teaching.

I went to Portland State University that summer and took a course called "Corrective Reading" from Dr. Colin Dunkeld, the man who gave me my first glimpse of what would become the whole language philosophy. Dr. Dunkeld shared with the class a project he had done on dialogue journals with a class of middle-school children. I was fascinated. Using the simple framework of a written dialogue between student and teacher, Dr. Dunkeld found that children dramatically improved their writing style and mechanics because of the motivation of a meaningful purpose for writing and the modeling of good written response from the teacher. I asked him if he would be interested in continuing his research using my classroom, and he readily accepted. For the next two years, Dr. Dunkeld spent a morning a week in my classroom and that of a colleague. He would observe in my classroom for an hour, then in my colleague's; then we had an hour while our children went to P.E. and music when we could debrief together. It was an ideal laboratory to try out our new ideas.

During my three years at Humboldt, I learned about teaching through my exploration of the writing process and the teaching of reading using real books. In those days, that was quite a radical way of thinking. Dr. Dunkeld gave me many books to read about this way of teaching, and I eagerly devoured them for new ideas and strategies. I can remember the fear and trepidation I felt as I stood before my class for the first time the fall of my second year of teaching, clutching Donald Graves' book *Writing: Teachers and Children at Work* open to the chapter "How to Survive Day One." Those were days of real experimentation and risk taking.

As this was going on for me, Kathy was exploring other new worlds, which led her to apply for and receive a Fulbright Teacher Exchange to London, England. She taught for a year at a primary school, working with four-year-olds in an all-day program. As part of the exchange program, she went to a weekend inservice course that included a workshop on the Storyline method. It was there that she met Steve Bell, one of the founders of the Storyline method. Kathy said of that first meeting, "I felt like I was having one of those experiences that happens only rarely, if ever, in one's teaching life, where everything I ever thought about teaching and learning was being challenged. I wanted to just sit in his pocket, so I could learn everything he knew. It really was a major paradigm shift." She then organized a study visit to Glasgow, Scotland, during a one-week holiday where she got a chance to visit Jordanhill College and several Scottish primary schools. Steve had introduced Kathy to something so intriguing that she just had to learn more.

In an attempt to explain the Storyline method to teachers back home, Kathy and Steve wrote an introduction for her to share on her return. The following is an excerpt from that introduction:

> The Storyline method is based on the theory that knowledge is complex and many layered, that learning is guided by one's prior knowledge and experience, and that learners construct their own meaning through action and experience. The Storyline creates a context for learning with the active involvement of the child. It provides tasks which arise from the context which the child sees as significant and meaningful within it. The Storyline gives the child opportunities to develop understanding and skills with the support of the context. The critical elements of the Storyline are:
>
> Setting the scene in a particular time and place
>
> People and/or animals
>
> A way of life to investigate
>
> Real problems to be solved

When Kathy returned home to Portland, she kept in touch with Steve, who invited her to come back to the U.K. to spend a year as a teaching fellow shadowing him at Jordanhill Teachers' College. She would work with the original team of staff tutors who had first developed Storyline twenty-five years before. Steve Bell, Sallie Harkness, and Fred Rendell took Kathy under their wing, and she began to learn about Storyline the only way anyone can: by doing it. She assisted as a tutor on courses for teachers throughout Europe, worked in classrooms, and observed in a variety of settings. When she came home from this trip she was a different person, and she was determined to share that difference with other teachers.

In her first year back from Scotland, she further explored Storyline in her own classroom as well as sharing it informally with anyone who was interested. I gathered a group of teachers from my school, and we spent an evening with Kathy, seeing her slides and talking to her about the possibilities that Storyline had to offer. She planned to bring Steve Bell to Portland the following summer to teach a few Storyline classes. Most of us were ready to sign up right then.

Based on the bits and pieces that Kathy had shared, my colleagues and I in fifth grade planned a Storyline topic together to help us teach American history. We had the kids make three groups of people: Native Americans, Europeans, and Africans. That part was really exciting. The kids loved making their characters and writing their biographies, and the excitement was just what we were looking for. Unfortunately, we hadn't thought through the whole thing—we had our characters, but we still had to figure out a way to get them to the colonies. We made ships and we acted out voyages. We painted Native American villages and we made artifacts. Thankfully, the year drew gracefully to a close so that we just stopped on the last day of school. I don't know how we ever would have ended the thing otherwise. It was a confused mess. Still, even with all the problems, my colleagues and I knew that we were onto something powerful. Despite all its flaws, this was one of the most motivating and exciting units we had ever done with our classes. The kids were so excited that they didn't want school to be over. That had never happened before!

That summer my colleagues and I took the class from Steve and Kathy, and together we wrote our first Storyline on the eruption of Mt. St. Helen's. Taking the class was a life-changing event for me. It wasn't until I put myself in the shoes of a learner and experienced a Storyline topic for myself that I understood how the whole thing fit together and made sense.

The Storyline topic we developed during the teachers' course involved the creation of a pet shop. We began by listing our favorite pets, and then we made them out of various collage materials. I remember Steve calling up one of the participants, handing her a felt pen and asking her to draw a penguin on the chart paper. She panicked, as most of us would, but Steve calmly began to ask her, "What is the basic shape of the body of a penguin? Where does the wing fit on the body? How large are a penguin's feet? Do penguins have mouths?" In doing this, Steve enabled the learner to draw out all of her prior knowledge, as well as helping her to see clearly what she didn't know. In the end, she produced a respectable penguin. Seeing her take the risk gave the rest of us the courage to tackle our own pet models.

Working in a group made the process much less intimidating because we could pool all of our experiences and come up with a knowledge base greater than any of us had on our own. (I remember one heated argument that lasted fifteen minutes about where the ear was on a squirrel!) Gradually, our pet shop came to life as we designed cages for our pets and displayed them on the walls of the conference room. When we made the pet shop employees, the whole thing really came together. We made magnificent full-body characters, wrote their biographies, and introduced them to the rest of the class. Spontaneously, relationships began to develop. Romances were started, intrigue grew, problems between people arose. We all were a part of this environment and we didn't want it to end. We cared about it because it was ours, and we had real reasons to do the things we were being asked to do. When money was found missing from the till, everyone plunged into the search for the culprit. A sick animal caused all of us to rethink our decision to not have a veterinarian on staff. At the end of our Storyline work, when we staged the grand opening of our pet shop, we all were wishing it didn't have to end so soon.

Through this personal experience I saw that the understanding of Storyline lies in *doing* it. It wasn't until I had to design a world, create a character, and live through incidents myself that I really understood the power of Storyline. The following fall Kathy and I started teaching Storyline classes for teachers, and we have been doing it ever since. Concurrent to all this, Kathy began working with Eileen Vopelak in Santa Barbara, California, and together they developed an innovative program to train summer-school teachers in Storyline, and then support them as they taught a five-week Storyline topic. The teachers had the advantage of doing a Storyline in a teaming situation, right when the class was fresh in their minds.

The demand for Storyline classes has only increased over the years. Every summer Steve Bell or Sallie Harkness has come over from Scotland to teach classes with us. Kathy first went to half-time teaching, so that she could fulfill the demands for classes. She then went on a leave of absence from her district to work with Storyline full-time. It has grown far bigger than any of us could have imagined.

For many years Kathy and I struggled with the issue of whether to write a book about Storyline. Every time we saw the need for it we came back to the same conclusion: Storyline is not something that can be taught in a book. It is something you have to do in order to understand. As a matter of fact, we have a hard time figuring out exactly what to call it: is it a method, a strategy, or a philosophy? Through our own journeys, we have come to realize that the answer is a paradoxical "yes." Storyline is a method: it is a way of working with children. There are principles to be followed, and techniques to be employed. Storyline is also a strategy: it provides a meaningful structure to integrate the curriculum. Yet, at the same time, Storyline is a philosophy: it is a way of looking at the learning process. It is a way of thinking about children. Perhaps the best way to represent the interplay of these three aspects of Storyline is with a Venn diagram—three circles overlapping each other, distinct yet interconnected.

Since this chapter was initially written, Kathy was stricken with ovarian cancer and passed away on July 9, 1994. Nothing could have prepared me for this tragedy. I see this book as a continuation of Kathy's vision for children started back in 1985, when she took her first Storyline class. We have her strength of vision and purpose to thank for the fact that the Storyline method has begun to transform the teaching/learning process here in the United States. This book is written with the hope that it will bring the Storyline idea to more teachers, and so provide children with a new and exciting way to learn.

This is not a how-to book. I hope that after reading it you will be inspired to take a Storyline class and begin your own discovery of working this way. I hope that sharing my experiences of Storyline and of how it transformed my own teaching may encourage you to try new ways of reaching the children you teach.

2 *The Philosophy*

I have always been concerned with integration and was initially attracted to Storyline because its approach to integration seemed new and different. First, a Storyline topic is written, like a good story, in a linear fashion. The key elements of any story—setting, characters, and plot—are all addressed. There is ownership on the part of the children as well as the teacher because they are working together to create the story. The story always begins with a key question, which is designed to draw out all of the collective knowledge in the class on the subject to be studied. This information is used to create the context in which the story will take place. This is perhaps the major difference between the Storyline method and thematic teaching: *Storyline begins by having the child create his or her own conceptual model first.* The role of imagination is critical here, for it is often through imagination that children fill in the gaps in their knowledge in the beginning of the topic study. This combination of prior knowledge and imagination is a powerful motivator that makes students feel that they are in control. In the process of using their prior knowledge, children begin to frame their own questions as they see what they don't know and what they need to know in order to complete the tasks at hand. These questions become the basis of future study. It is at the end of the Storyline topic that the children compare what they have created to its real-world equivalent.

A Storyline is written as a series of episodes. The first episode often begins with a key question that starts children thinking about the setting for their story. From the brainstorm list that results from the discussion, children begin to bring the setting to life. Perhaps a large frieze will be constructed on a wall in the classroom. As the children begin to establish this setting based on their collective knowledge of the subject, the story takes on a life of its own. The power in the setting lies in the fact that it is unique to the class and it contains input from each member of the class.

In a well-constructed Storyline, the children will ask the key question before the teacher does because they understand the internal logic of the story. When the setting is completed it becomes evident that people are needed. Characters in a Storyline can take many forms. Sometimes, small cutout figures are made using fabric scraps, glue, bric-a-brac, sequins, buttons, pipe cleaners, and yarn. The characters are brought to life as biographies are written, relationships are explored, and the people take their place in the environment. A way of life is explored for these characters and jobs are created, schedules written, basic needs addressed.

Inevitably, once this collective context is living and breathing, incidents occur where the characters have to respond to a need or deal with an emergency. A robbery might take place, a fire could break out, a disaster could occur. Each of these incidents provides the opportunity to build in specific pieces of required content. These may be acted out, drawn as cartoons, read as reader's theatre, performed with puppets, or written as stories. An incident might also point to the need for children to do some research in order to solve the problem. Frequently, there are a series of incidents, some teacher initiated, some child initiated. The teacher-initiated incidents most often arise from a goal within the curriculum that needs to be addressed. An outbreak of food poisoning in the class restaurant could lead to a study of good, healthy food preparation procedures, or even a study of airborne diseases and germs, depending on the ages of the children.

Most Storyline topics conclude with a celebration or an event to mark the completion of the study: a grand opening, a performance, a visit from a local expert, or a field trip to an appropriate site. This event helps children to summarize the experience, draw conclusions, share what they have learned. It also gives them the opportunity to compare their creation with the real world. Because of their personal experience they are intensely curious about how things are done in the real world. Oftentimes they prefer their own solutions to a particular problem when comparing it to the real thing! Sometimes a topic book is made in which all of the pertinent work that has been done during the unit is bound into a large book to be kept as a memento of the study. This book can also be used as a portfolio for assessment purposes.

Just this afternoon I worked with my mixed-age class of third and fourth graders on our radio station Storyline. We were constructing the storefront that would eventually house our radio station, KPIC: Kids Put In Charge. These two scenarios give a window into the possibilities for learning that are contained within the context of a Storyline topic.

One of my students, Adam, is a classic learning-disabled child. He has a very short attention span and never sits still. He spent an hour and a half working on a tree to landscape the building. One of the children working with him made a bird's nest with a robin sitting on the edge. Adam designed an elaborate overhang of leaves that was cantilevered over the nest using yarn so that the robins would stay dry when it rained. It happened to be pouring rain at the time, and he was genuinely concerned for the safety of these little creatures. This work took him an uncharacteristically long time, and it was self-initiated and self-monitored.

Andranique, a strong-willed perfectionist, worked the whole time on the checkerboard back of the booths in the window of the cafe in the same building as the radio station. She had meticulously sketched the details of this cafe when we had gone on our walking trip to choose a vacant storefront for KPIC. She wanted to paint the checkerboard and she tried to do it freehand. The difficulty arose when she had to paint the same checkerboard pattern in two different windowpanes. She just couldn't get the two panes properly aligned to her satisfaction. By the time she had finished, we had covered up three unsuccessful attempts with fresh paper. She refused to stop because it was important to her to get it right.

Adam is a fourth grader, and Andranique is a third grader. They represent the passion that children have for studying in a way that empowers them to create their own learning environment and to seek out the answers to real questions that they care about, questions they have posed because they really want to know.

For the teacher, this method offers a structure for making the *teachable moment* a daily occurrence in the classroom. Teachers are amazed at the potential they have to explore the curriculum they are required to teach, in a way that is motivating and exciting.

The teacher, in writing the topic outline, controls the direction that the study will take in much the same way that a map gives direction to a destination. However, it is up to the children to actually take the journey and bring the story to life. Through the richness of their own collective experience and imagination children explore, in depth, a topic that has real relevance in the world today. From this microcosm the children can generalize to the rest of the world. For example, the children might study the Civil War by creating a town in Indiana that was involved in the war. They would study the war through the eyes of their own character that they have created. They would see the larger picture of the war as someone who personally lived through it. This would give them insight into war in general, and some of the real human reasons that people end up trying to use war to solve their problems. Their personal experience in the Storyline becomes a template for studying any war or conflict. A more traditional study of another conflict in history now has a context.

Storyline is truly a constructivist philosophy, and as such I have found it helpful to articulate its uniqueness through a set of principles. These principles help to give a language to the qualities that make the Storyline method a unique and distinctive way of working.

Principles of the Storyline Method

Principles guide practice and shape planning, thinking, and assessment. Without them, Storyline could be reduced to a set of clever art activities planned to enrich a traditional subject-by-subject curriculum.

The European Association for Educational Design, or EED, is the organization of Storyline educators that sponsors the international Golden Circle Storyline Conference. Every eighteen months, the key educators in those countries using the method get together to share ideas and support one another. I have used their set of principles as a basis for those listed below. These principles highlight the distinctiveness of the Storyline method and are important guidelines to remember when planning and implementing a Storyline topic.

- *The Principle of Story.* Story is a central part of human experience. Our history, religion, and heritage have all been passed from generation to generation through stories for thousands of years. When we seek to understand the world around us or the culture of a people, we look to stories to enlighten us. Stories provide children with a predictable, linear structure and a meaningful context for learning what we are trying to teach. Storyline uses this powerful principle to teach required curriculum in a way that closely mirrors real life.
- *The Principle of Anticipation.* A good story draws us into its spell as we predict what is coming and we anticipate its unfolding with joy and excitement. All children want to know "What's going to happen next?" They follow the story from episode to episode, eager to see where it will go. Anticipation is also present at the end of a story when children ask, "What is the next Storyline going to be about?" Anticipation ensures that learning goes on all the time, whether in school or at home, because children are involved in a process that they feel a part of. They are thinking about the story all the time, and bringing their thoughts and ideas with them to each class session eager to contribute to the growing story unfolding around them.
- *The Principle of the Teacher's Rope.* This principle refers to the critical partnership between teacher and student in a Storyline topic. Storyline is also referred to as collaborative story making because

of the balance between teacher control and student control. The teacher at all times holds the rope that is the actual "Storyline" planned to include specific curricular goals. The magic of a rope is that it is flexible and allows for numerous bends and twists and knots while moving from one end to the other. This gives children their control. Still, the rope is the road that is being traveled and in spite of the unexpected detours and diversions, the children follow the path the teacher designed and learn the curriculum the teacher had planned.

- *The Principle of Ownership.* This is surely the most powerful motivator for children. Children feel responsibility, pride, and enthusiasm for projects in which they play a substantive role. Storyline honors children by beginning with the key question "What is a ____________?" or "What do you think a ____________ is like?" This idea of starting by building the children's conceptual model first says that children are not empty vessels waiting to be filled. Collectively they know far more about a given subject than they do as individuals. In my experience, my children often know more than I do about any given subject. By taking the children's conceptual model seriously and visually bringing it to life in the classroom, we provide the fuel that drives the entire Storyline topic.
- *The Principle of Context.* This principle is closely linked to the principle of story. New learning must be linked to previous knowledge. Children build their understanding by going from the known to the unknown. Context provides children the reason for learning what we want them to learn. Since a Storyline topic mirrors real life, the context is familiar and children see its relationship to their own lives. The linear, predictable structure of the story is also a context they understand. Children research, practice skills, and assimilate new knowledge because the story demands it, and because they care about it. They have a genuine need to know.
- *The Structure Before Activity Principle.* By asking children to build their conceptual model first we give them the chance to push their prior knowledge to its edges. When they have reached this point we know that they will frame their own questions and go about trying to find the answers. Children need to discover what they don't know by articulating what they do know and to see the gaps. Once this has been done, children need to be given structures that will enable them to find out what they want to know and to present what they discover. The teacher provides an

appropriate structure for creating a frieze, doing research, writing a report, doing a presentation, or creating a character so that all children have a point of reference or starting point. This structure equals freedom for those children who don't have the skills to accomplish the task on their own. Those who do possess the skills have the freedom to use the structure if they choose, or to diverge from it. This principle supports the belief that all children can accomplish what is being asked of them, provided they are given the necessary structure first.

This list of six principles provides a framework to keep in mind while planning a topic and implementing it in the classroom. I use them as filters to focus my work with children. As you read the chapters that describe the five different Storyline topics, look for these principles in action.

3 *The Structure*

Storyline is a constructivist way of working and cannot be fully understood without actually doing it yourself. Therefore it may seem like I am putting the cart before the horse to discuss the structure of the Storyline method at the beginning. In an ideal situation, the reader would have had the opportunity to take the Storyline course before reading this book. Then the constructivist cycle of experience followed by reflection and ending with theory could be applied in the book. Since this is not possible for all readers, it is important to provide the larger context so that teachers will see how Storyline relates to the curriculum as a whole.

For those who are anxious to get on with the chapters that describe some topics as they occurred in my classroom, I would encourage you to skip this chapter and go on to the next, "The Hotel." After reading through this topic and seeing some of the pictures, you can then come back to this chapter and get filled in on some of the nuts and bolts. For those who want to see behind the scenes before you plow ahead, read on!

The sections of this chapter deal with four critical issues: scheduling, planning, teaming, and grouping. These are the components of the Storyline structure that set it apart from other methods of integration. Many people who take a Storyline class and then go back to their schools to try a Storyline topic for themselves find that they get bogged down because they haven't restructured their total program and redesigned it to fit the Storyline model. In this situation, teachers find that Storyline takes too much time, and they either abandon it or don't give it the time that it needs. If teachers hang onto their old schedules and try to squeeze Storyline in, Storyline becomes an add-on and not a new structure for teaching the curriculum. In my classroom I have restructured according to the ideas I am about to share.

Daily/Weekly/Yearly Schedules

The question often arises as to how much time is devoted to Storyline work throughout the year. I am quick to point out that Storyline does not take up my whole day. I use my morning time to teach a math, reading, and writing program. These are taught as workshops with lots of activities and opportunities for student choice. Most of my afternoon time is spent working on the Storyline topic. This works out to between one and two hours a day (see Fig. 3–1).

I try to make sure that I give my Storyline topic at least six hours a week. This time allocation is flexible because there are times in the Storyline when more time is needed, and other times when we can go a few days without working. The demands on the schedule dictate how the time is broken up, but I have discovered that spending less than six hours a week causes the story to bog down, and the children's enthusiasm for the topic quickly fades. There must always be a sense of expectation on the part of the children; they must feel that they are making progress toward a goal, whether that be a field trip, a performance, a sharing time, or a visit from an expert.

You will note in my weekly plan there are only five hours allotted for "Project Time," which is my Storyline time. This is because I often use my regular writing, reading, or math time to teach a skill or conduct an activity that is related to the Storyline topic. For example, if I am going to plan an activity in the Storyline in which the children design a scale model, then I will teach area and scale during my math time. In this way the Storyline is often infused into every aspect of the curriculum. In writers' workshop the children will often be writing about the Storyline or working on a specific piece of reflective writing. They choose to do this writing during workshop because they are so involved in the topic that they want to use as much time as they can to work on it. As you can imagine, this kind of passion for the topic dramatically improves many of the children's writing skills.

One of the powerful benefits of the Storyline method is that it provides a meaningful context for children to practice the skills we want them to know. I can teach the elements of how to write a business letter, and children can take a test showing that they know all of the parts of a business letter. But in a Storyline, they have the opportunity to demonstrate their deeper understanding because they can determine a need for a business letter, write one, and actually use it for their own purposes. This removes the drudgery; it is practice for a reason within a context that makes sense to the child.

I plan on doing three Storyline topics a year. The first will take me up to the winter holiday. The second takes us up to spring vacation, and the

Friday	Thursday	Wednesday	Tuesday	Monday	Date:
DOL/DOG	DOL/DOG	DOL/DOG	DOL/DOG	DOL/DOG	8:35 to 8:50
	Music	P.E.	Library	Music	8:50 to 9:20
Math	Science 9:40-10:25 Math 10:25-10:45	Math	Math	Math	9:20 to 10:45
Playtime	Playtime	Playtime	Playtime	Playtime	10:45 to 11:00
Writing	Reading SSR	Writing	Reading SSR 11:00 Roberta	Writing	11:00 to 11:50
Read Aloud	Read Aloud	Read Aloud	Read Aloud	Read Aloud	11:50 to 12:10
Lunch/Recess	Lunch/Recess	Lunch/Recess	Lunch/Recess	Lunch/Recess	12:10 to 1:00
			Science 1:00-1:45	1:00 Susie	1:00 to 1:30
Storyline	Swimming at Matt Dishman (lessons 2:00-2:30) Homework:	Early Dismissal Homework:	Storyline Homework:	Storyline Homework:	1:30 to 2:45
Assignments			Assignments	Assignments	2:45 to 3:00

Figure 3–1. My weekly plan book

third goes to the end of the year. There have been years when I have done as many as five Storylines, and others when I only did two. I look at my curriculum and determine what goes together and makes sense to accomplish in each Storyline topic. For example, the first Storyline that I did with my class this past fall was The Presidential Campaign. I was teaching fifth grade, and I knew that my social studies curriculum was United States history and government. I thought it made sense to take advantage of the 1996 presidential election and use it as the vehicle for a Storyline with a social studies focus.

Each Storyline usually has one major focus area and two other areas I will do some important work with. The Presidential Campaign had a social studies focus. Language arts was one of the minors because the children would write and deliver speeches, research and write party platforms, and read lots of campaign literature and news articles about the issues. The other minor for this Storyline was career education. The children would apply for jobs at the campaign headquarters of the two parties they created, and they would need to perform the duties and responsibilities of those jobs.

In the winter I did a Storyline topic on the new school playground. I worked cooperatively with a teacher in a mixed-age first- and second-grade class. We researched, designed, fund-raised, and got a new playground built for our school. This Storyline had a science and health focus. We did a lot of design work and we looked at the health and safety issues related to playground design. There was an art minor because of all the drawing and model building. There was also a math minor because of the many calculations needed to figure out how much material and how to use the space we have available. My fifth graders worked closely with the first and second graders to help them with the more difficult aspects of the project. That dictated that my students needed to learn certain things ahead of time, so they could teach them to the younger children. It provided rich learning opportunities in both directions.

This spring I planned a Storyline topic based on the picture book *Miss Rumphius* by Barbara Cooney. This had a language-arts major and minors in geography and art. I like to do Storylines that have an element of fantasy and adventure in the spring, so the children can celebrate the year together and have the chance to imaginatively use all of the skills they have worked on all year. In this Storyline, the children explored the life of Miss Rumphius, following her travels around the world, and grappling with her charge to do something to make the world more beautiful. We all went home for the summer with baby lupines to plant in our gardens.

Planning a Storyline Topic

Planning a topic is very different from the kind of planning I do for my reading, writing, and math programs. Although I do long-range planning in the fall to determine the scope of what I want to cover during the year, I am able to plan these subjects week to week or unit by unit. In a Storyline topic the planning is definitely front-ended. I have to have a chunk of time, usually a good eight to ten hours, to work through the whole Storyline from beginning to end. Without this prior planning I run the risk of losing the story in my day-to-day work with the children. The finished Storyline is the teacher's rope that I referred to earlier, and I need to have that clearly mapped out before I begin. This requires me to really know my state and district curriculum guidelines, so that I am clear about what I need to teach. Only then can I design a Storyline topic that will meet those goals. I have to decide the concepts and processes I will be teaching in the Storyline because these help me to decide on my major and minor areas of focus.

Planning a Storyline topic is a two-step process. First, I must map out the story an episode at a time, and design the key questions that will start each of these episodes. The episodes, like the chapters in a book, move the story along to its logical conclusion. The key question acts as the syntactic trampoline that sends us off into the story. Key questions are big and broad. They are designed to allow children to think about everything they know about a subject. A good key question must provoke a rich and wide array of responses that can be recorded and used as a knowledge base in the activities of the topic. In the five chapters describing different topics, I have italicized the key questions so that you can see how they help to give the topic direction and how they are used to gather together the children's prior knowledge.

When writing the episodes I pay careful attention to three critical areas. First, I need to decide how the topic will begin. Will I start with a letter or an extract? Will the children simply discuss a key question and begin building? Second, I need to decide what the concluding episode will be. Will we visit the real thing? Perhaps we will invite an expert in? Will there be a presentation or performance for parents and family? Finally, I need to build in a reflection piece at the conclusion of the Storyline topic. Will the children make a topic book? Will they write a reflective piece summarizing all that they have learned? Will they complete a cumulative journal throughout the Storyline?

Once I have written the episodes and key questions, I can go back and fill in the remaining four columns on the planning form I use. I must decide what activities I will have the children do within each episode,

The Hotel

Storyline Episodes	Key Questions	Possible Activities	Class Organization	Resources	Goals/Obj
1. The Hotel	What is a hotel? Who needs a hotel? What hotels are there in (your city)?	Discuss hotels create a brainstorming list; write letters of inquiry to local hotels. Design exterior of hotel on paper. Create frieze of hotel exterior; Name the hotel; take walking tour of local hotels noting architectural details and features	Whole Class Groups of 4 Whole Class	Sugar paper, colored pencils, scissors, card, blue tack, fabic scraps, foil paper, colored cellophane, etc.	English: AT1, 4C, 5A, 5B, AT2, AT3, 4A, 4B, 4E, AT4, 4A, AT5, 5A, 5B, 5C
2. The Guests	Who would use a hotel and why? What might draw people to (city) at Christmas time?	Create hotel residents making small people, display on frieze; Create a biography form for guests	Groups of 4 Whole Class	Bio form: name, address, phone #, age, occupation, family members, religious affiliation, hobbies, reason for using the hotel	Art: AT1, a, b, c, d, AT2, b Technology: AT 4A, 4C, 4D, AT2, 4A, 4B, 4C, 4, 5A, 5B, 5C, AT3, 4A, 4B 4C, 4D, 5A, 5B, 5C, 5D, AT4, 4A, 4B, 4C, 4D, 5
3. A Guest Room	What are the necessary features of a hotel guest room? Are there certain design criteria that must be considered? Does a hotel need different kinds and sizes of rooms?	Discuss features, etc. creating a brainstorm list. Design a set of criteria for hotel rooms. Decide on the different kinds of rooms that need to be designed. Make blueprints of rooms. Design box models of rooms. Present room designs to a design board from another class.	Whole Class Groups of 4	Drawing paper, boxes for models, clipboards for design team, materials to create models - fabric, glue, scissors, assorted papers, rulers, foil, etc.	
4. The Hotel Staff	Who works at a hotel? What would his/her daily routine be like?	Discuss hotel staff and duties. Write a timetable for a day at work for a staff member. Create a staff portrait to hang in the hotel.	Whole Class Groups of 2 Individual	A-4 backing paper sugar paper, glue, paints	

The Hotel

Storyline Episodes	Key Questions	Possible Activities	Class Organization	Resources	Goals/ Obj
5. The Incidents	What could happen to your guests at the hotel?	Discuss possible incidents. Two groups work together on presenting a skit of an incident.	Whole Class Groups of 8	Chart paper, musical instruments, props	
6. Develop- ments	What arrangements must be made for safety at the hotel?	Discuss the need for safety regulatons. Write wall sign to display safety rules for different places in the hotel.	Whole Class Groups of 4	Large paper, backing paper, sample of safety regulations	
7. A Visit	How does our hotel compare with the real thing?	A local hotel manager comes to see thehotel plans and answer questions.	Whole Class		

Figure 3–2. Topic outline for The Hotel Storyline

how I will group the children during these activities, what resources I will need, and lastly, what goals I am working on and what assessment tools I will use when appropriate. In The Hotel plan (Fig. 3–2), goals are written as a list of numbers preceded by the letters AT, or Attainment Targets, and are the specific goals within the English National Curriculum that I was teaching during the course of the topic. The goals are not written with a one-to-one correspondence to the activities, but reflect the scope of goals that are covered during the course of the study. I was purposely specific because I wanted to assure myself that I was systematically teaching the curriculum I was responsible for.

Once I have this plan completed I have the road map for the next two or three months. It doesn't look like much, but it tells me where I am going and what I have to accomplish. All I need to do from week to week is predict how far we will get, and refer back to the plan from time to time to make sure that I am moving along at a pace that will get me through the topic in the time I have planned for it. Now that I have done several Storyline topics in my classroom, I find it helpful to write an estimated number of days next to the activities, so that I have an idea how long I might be spending on any one activity. This is always kept flexible, but it helps me to not get bogged down in one activity for too long.

When I am ready to actually teach the Storyline topic, I sit down with my finished topic outline and my weekly planbook and I lay out exactly what we will be doing on each day of the first week. At the end of this week, I usually have a good sense of the pace of the Storyline, and I can then go ahead and put the next four weeks of the topic outline into my weekly planbook. This takes me to about the middle of the topic. When I reach this point in the Storyline, I have found it useful to look ahead and decide when I want to have my concluding event and set a date. Then, using my weekly planbook, I work backward until I get to the present. This way I make sure that I am only doing the things that are most important. It is easy for the topic to get sidetracked and lose momentum. I often find that I have to skip some of the activities that I wrote in my topic outline in order to finish the topic in time. This forces me to stay on task, and keep my focus on the important concepts and processes that I want the children to learn. It also helps me to keep the story moving.

Teaming

The Storyline method is a collaborative way of working that allows teachers and children to share the ownership of the learning in the classroom. In the same way, it is a way of working that requires lots of collegial support between teachers. All the Storyline topics in this book were done in collaboration with other teachers. I needed the support, advice, and perspectives of my colleagues because this is a demanding way of teaching. It involves taking risks and giving kids control. I have been successful with Storyline in large part because I have not been alone.

The importance of teaming begins in the planning stages. I have never written a Storyline topic by myself. Writing a topic is such a dynamic process that it requires more than one head working on it. When I am actually doing a Storyline, I always make sure that I have at least one other teacher who I can talk to on a daily basis—if not a teacher doing the same Storyline then a teacher at another grade level.

Grouping

There is one guideline that I remember whenever I am trying to decide how to group children for an activity in a Storyline topic: *Let the activity determine the grouping*. Some activities naturally lend themselves to individual work. This is particularly true if you want a formal piece for evaluation at the end. Other activities benefit from pairs of children working together. I find that when I have children doing research within a topic it helps to have two working on the same project. Still other activities require small groups of three, four, or five. When we are working on building the frieze or making box models, small groups, each with a different task, work best. Finally, the initial brainstorm related to the key question and the final discussion prior to writing a reflective piece are best done as a whole group.

Determining the size of the group is only one issue; you must also decide how the groups will be chosen and how long the groups will work together. Both of these issues require careful consideration.

In the beginning of the year I am very cautious about letting the children choose the groups. I do not know them very well and I haven't been able to see how well they work together. In my experience, children do not always make wise choices about whom they work with. I tend to choose the groups at first, so that I can get a good balance of boys and girls, abilities, and ethnic backgrounds. I explain to the children that I am doing this with the understanding that I will be letting them make this choice for themselves later in the year. I don't want to take for granted that the children will know how to work in a group and cooperate. I figure that I will be spending a good portion of my early Storyline work in the fall teaching cooperative learning skills. I am always on the lookout for problems, and when I see them in a group I stop the whole class and we talk about ways to resolve the situation. Sometimes, I have to be directive and remove a difficult child from a group. If this happens, I keep that child with me until he or she is ready to try again. Then I set up a time to check back with the group to see how things are going.

By midyear, I am usually ready to let children select their own groups. I start this process by having children brainstorm what makes an effective group member. We narrow this down to a list of four or five qualifications. When the children have chosen their groups, I have them sit in a circle and share their willingness to work together according to the qualifications determined by the class. Then, if there is a problem in a group, we have a system in place for identifying the problem and working toward a solution.

On occasion I have allowed a child who refused to cooperate to work by him- or herself. The sheer boredom of trying to complete a group project on your own usually has that person happily back in the group within a few days!

Half of the children I now teach have been in my classroom since third grade. They know me well, and they know my expectations for group behavior. More important, they know each other well, and they know who they can work with. These children always get to choose their groups unless I feel that they are making a poor choice, and then I reserve the right to make a switch. If it comes to that, the children usually don't argue because we have discussed the problem beforehand and they know the limits. I see self-selection of groups as the ultimate goal in all group work.

It is important in choosing groups to bear in mind the amount of time the groups will be together. Any group will run into problems if they work together too long. I think it is a good idea to change groups for each episode, except in rare cases where the story requires that they stay together for a longer period of time.

In the Space Adventure Storyline I write about in Chapter 5, the children had to stay in their work groups for the whole design process of creating the interior of the space bubble. Cooperation and teamwork were a major emphasis of this Storyline. We discussed the importance of each group member in reaching the goal and the fact that all groups working together as a whole were needed to get us safely into space.

Usually variety in grouping helps to keep the story alive and moving. The children anticipate new groups to work in. It also helps children who may find themselves in a difficult group to realize that they will only be in that group for a short period of time to accomplish a specific task.

4 *The Hotel*

The Storyline topic that follows was done during the 1992–1993 school year. I was on a Fulbright Teacher Exchange in Colchester, England, at St. George's County Junior School. St. George's is located in a working-class neighborhood of Victorian council houses, subsidized housing for low-income people. The school, built in 1903, houses eight classrooms of thirty to thirty-five students, ages seven to eleven. I was teaching year six, which is equivalent to fifth grade, and I had thirty-two students. During November of that school year, I had attended a two-day Storyline seminar in Glasgow, Scotland, taught by Steve Bell and Fred Rendell. My deputy head teacher (vice principal) had accompanied me at the request of my head teacher (principal), who was hoping to offer Storyline training to the whole staff in the winter. My deputy head was so enthusiastic about Storyline that he came back and started working on The Hotel with me after the Christmas holiday. I taught a course for the staff in January and February, and we did an all-school topic called Capital Tours in the spring. Capital Tours involved students planning a family vacation to four European capitals.

The Hotel topic was done over a three-month period, from January through March. Generally, we worked on the topic for two hours every afternoon. This varied according to the tasks at hand. When we were preparing to perform our skits we worked on them for several full days. The children negotiated for more time when they felt it was necessary. During the rest of the day I conducted a regular math program, a writers' workshop, and a novel-based reading program.

The Hotel topic had a major curriculum focus in math and design technology, with minor focuses in health and language arts.

I have divided the Storyline into episodes and given the approximate time that I spent on each so that you can get an idea of the structure I talked about in Chapter 3. You may want to refer to the topic outline in Chapter 3 when you come across an italicized key question, so that you can see how the topic is developing in relationship to the topic outline. You will notice that the actual working out of the topic in the classroom does not directly correspond to the topic outline. Some of the episodes are in a different order, and some of the key questions are slightly different. As the Storyline progressed I changed the plans so that they fit with what the children were developing. Although I never lost hold of the teacher's rope, I allowed the Storyline to respond to the needs of the children. This is why the original topic outline is always a guide that must be modified as the topic unfolds in the classroom.

Episode One The Hotel *(3 weeks)*

I am sitting on the rug with my fifth graders, when I pose the initial question, *What is a hotel?* They look at me quizzically, wondering if this is for real. Eventually someone volunteers a response. "It's a place where people go to stay when they are away from home." Then, another: "It's got a swimming pool and a fancy restaurant!" More follow: "Famous people stay in hotels and if you go there sometimes you get to see them." "A hotel is where you go when you're on vacation and your mom doesn't want to cook or make the beds."

"Hold it just a minute," I say. "Can you go back. I've got 'A hotel is where you go when you're on vacation. . . .'" "And your mom doesn't want to cook or make the beds," they answer.

"Thanks," I reply. "I wanted to be sure I got your words right on the chart." I continue taking down the children's words until we have a full piece of chart paper. "Isn't it amazing all the things that we know about hotels?" I ask them. "We have the opportunity to design a hotel for Colchester, so I wanted you to have a good idea of what one was. I want you to go off in groups of four and talk about what a new hotel for Colchester might look like. Find a quiet space in the room where you won't bother other groups. When you think you have a good idea, send someone from your group up to me and I will give you a piece of chart paper so you can draw a sketch of the facade, or the front of your hotel. When each group has finished their sketch we will share them with the class to see what we like best in each one."

The groups are listed on a chart that I have posted, and the children find their group members and head for a space in the room to begin their discussions. I wander from group to group, listening in on the conversation, asking a question where it seems appropriate, keeping silent when things are going well. This is a very messy time. I don't feel that I am in control and it takes me a while to take the pulse of the class. I am periodically interrupted by someone needing a piece of paper to begin sketching. I find that I am constantly having to do a balancing act. If I spend too long with one group, then I lose touch with the rest of the class. It is easy for me to be unaware that a group is in trouble until there is a scene.

As the groups finish their sketches, I hang them around the room, and the groups prepare to present their ideas to the class. Eventually, we agree on a time when everyone must be finished and the presentations will start. Usually this takes place the following day so that groups that need more time can take things home. Some groups must be content with the fact that they have to share an unfinished sketch.

Each group shares what they have designed and the class takes time to give specific feedback about what they like. Give-and-take goes on as groups view each other's work and ideas spread around the room.

"Your windows are really neat. I like the way they face the river."

"That's a really cool awning over the entrance. It would be nice to have that when it was raining."

"The gardens are really colorful. That makes the whole place seem cheerful."

"I love the helicopter pad on the roof. It would be good if you needed a quick way to get to the airport."

I act as recorder, writing down all of the comments for each group so that when we are through we have a list of all the things we like from each sketch. I have added my comments too, as a member of the class. This is the stage of the Storyline where we are building our conceptual model of a hotel, and it is critical that I draw out all of the ideas from each group. The hotel we build will be the context for our Storyline so it is important that everyone has input in this early design stage.

Then I tell them that the next step is to look for common elements and come up with a "Best-Parts List," which will include all of the things we want to have in the hotel we are going to build. What are the things that you see in a number of different designs that you want to be sure and include in the hotel that we are going to build? I ask them.

When the "Best-Parts List" is completed, we categorize it so that we can determine work parties for building the hotel. The windows and doors group, the sign group, the gardens group, the entrance group, the background group, and the restaurant group are what we come up with. Each group is limited to a maximum of five people so that all of the groups have enough people in them. Children sign up for the group they want to work in. I stress the fact that they need to have a couple of choices in mind as they may not get their first choice.

As most of the groups meet to plan what they want to do, I meet with the background group so that they can quickly put up the outline of the hotel. This is crucial for the other groups so that they can have an idea of scale for the things they are going to create. This takes a while, and so the other groups do preliminary drawings of their ideas in order that each member of the group understands what they are going to try and accomplish. Once the hotel outline is up, the rest of the groups can come up and judge how large or small they will have to make their things. The background group can now concentrate on filling in the details that will show the building materials, and put their finishing touches on the building itself. In this case, the Aquarium Hotel was built of gray stone.

The idea of scale is very difficult for some of the children, so I pull a few children and work with them separately until I feel that they have enough of an understanding to make their contribution to the hotel.

The hotel takes shape on a large bulletin board in the room. It extends above and below the actual board because this allows the hotel to have the grand scale that the children want. Children experiment with 3-D, and parts of the hotel stand out from the wall. A table is placed in front of the board and part of the hotel extends onto the tabletop to show the drive and a waterfront.

The supplies for building the hotel are many and varied: butcher paper, various shades of paper painted with tempera, cloth scraps, cardboard, colored cellophane, foil, sequins, glitter, wallpaper samples, artificial plants, moss, Popsicle sticks, brown paper sacks, fake fur, Styrofoam, and anything else that has been scrounged by me or the kids.

I am acting as facilitator, giving advice, when asked, or finding supplies that aren't available in the room. Much of my time is spent running around the building locating special supplies or taking children to use the phone or the copy machine. This whole process is messy, noisy, and chaotic. The room is loud, but the class is usually productive. When I think things are getting out of hand, we stop and make adjustments. When a child feels it is out of hand we do the same.

The learning taking place during this time is rich and varied, and I am not at all aware of everything that is happening. I do my best to check in regularly with each group to see what they have discovered or to offer a hint or an idea if they seem stuck. I want to help them take their ideas and figure out a way to make those ideas come alive in the frieze. The vision of the hotel as it unfolds in the class is a powerful motivator for all of us. Everyone wants to do work of the highest quality because everyone sees the wonderful work being done by the others.

During this construction period, the children run up against some blocks in their knowledge and ask for help. We plan a walking trip to visit some of the hotels in the area to look at architectural details. Some children borrow the audio-visual catalog to order films, videos, or filmstrips that might help. Children spontaneously do research on their own, taking trips to the public library or visiting a hotel and bringing back brochures. I keep my mouth shut and let the children come to me with the questions. Then I help them figure out where to get answers.

This creation stage takes a good two weeks, working two hours a day. I am constantly checking in with groups to see what they are doing and where they are going. When a group finishes early they help another group, because some tasks are more time-consuming than others. Some groups will begin a new task that will help us later on in the topic. A sign for the hotel is designed. Pockets to hold word bank cards are made, and children start to build a vocabulary bank to describe the hotel. These words help to build the atmosphere of the hotel. Later on, children will use these words as they write about the hotel and events that happen in it.

At last we reach a point where we can say that the hotel is finished. As we stand back and admire our efforts, someone blurts out, "What are we going to call it?" This is a natural question to ask, inspired by the internal logic of the story. Our hotel is coming to life, and it makes sense that it needs a name.

"You are quite right," I say. "Our hotel doesn't have a name. Does anyone have any ideas?" A chart of suggested names is started, and it is soon filled. Everyone has a case to make for his or her name. The Golden Eagle, The Grand Hotel, The Silver Swan, The Aquarium Hotel, and The Water's Edge are a few of the suggestions. We vote and narrow it down to three so that we can finally pick a winning name.

Figure 4–1. Facade of the Aquarium Hotel

Our hotel, The Aquarium, is quite impressive. It is a stone structure, two stories high with an elegant entryway with large sculpted fish over the doorway. Two smartly dressed footmen stand on either side of the doors to welcome guests. The restaurant, The Comfortable Restaurant, is attached to the hotel by a covered walkway. There are balconies outside every window with flower boxes and beautiful blue draperies in the full-length windows. We meet as a class in front of The Aquarium to celebrate our accomplishments and to admire our finished product. Each work group has the opportunity to share their contribution and to hear specific praise from the rest of the class. A few things aren't quite right, and we make arrangements to change those at another time. Unlike a mural, which is finished and then left alone, the frieze is an active environment that the class uses and refers to constantly throughout the Storyline. The principle of ownership is written on the faces of all of the children as they stand back to admire the Aquarium Hotel.

Episode 2 The Staff *(2 weeks)*

"We now have a beautiful hotel on the waterfront in Colchester," I tell the students, "But it seems to me that there is something missing. Does anyone have any idea what it might be?"

"We have a hotel, but we don't have any people!" pipes up an enthusiastic student. The child knows that the story needs people if it is going to progress, and so he naturally takes us into the next episode of the Storyline.

"I couldn't have said it better myself," I add. "We could never open The Aquarium Hotel because we don't have any people to run it. *Who do you think works in a hotel?*"

"Maids."

"Bellboys."

"A security guard."

"A manager."

"A chef."

The list continues until we have a long list of everyone who might work in a hotel, including the helicopter pilot! Would a real hotel have a helicopter pilot? Perhaps not, but it is this interplay between reality and imagination that keeps the story alive and exciting. It is one of the ways that the children are making the story their own. What is important is that the children care about this hotel because it belongs to them.

"We are going to create the people who run The Aquarium Hotel," I tell them, "but first we must decide which of the people on our list are really essential to the running of the hotel. In other words, those people that we absolutely couldn't run the hotel without." I go through the list with the children and star every person that they feel is indispensable and then say to them, "Now I want you to come up and put your name by the person that you would like to create. We have to make sure that we make the essential people, but after that we can have more than one kind of some of our employees."

The children come up and sign their names by the person that they want to make. I give the children a simple structure for making a portrait of a person, saying, "I want you to create a staff photo to be hung in the lobby of the hotel so that the guests will know who works at The Aquarium. I don't want you to draw this photo or portrait, I want you to build it. Start with the shape of the head. What do you think a head is shaped like?"

"An egg!" a student replies.

"Great!" I say. "Cut out your egg shape so that it fills this piece of paper. You can leave a little room at the bottom for a neck and shoulders if you want, but I want these faces to be large enough to be seen easily in the lobby."

I continue to talk the children through the construction of the faces. We discuss where the eyes are in the head, the nose, and the mouth, and where the ears should be. I share a technique with them for making the features 3-D by cutting them in half and folding them before gluing, leaving part of the feature sticking out. Here is the structure-before-activity principle in action: If I had simply told the children to make a face, many of them would have thrown up their hands in despair and said they couldn't do it. Instead, I gave them a structure for making a face so that everyone had a tool for being successful. The children with artistic ability are very loose with my structure and the children, like myself, who have no confidence, stick closely to the structure. In all cases the structure equals freedom. Everyone can make a portrait.

The children are not in groups because this is an individual project; they sit where they please. The making of the hotel staff takes several days because children must make their portrait, mount it on a background, and then design a frame to go around it. I choose a wall near the hotel frieze to put up the staff portraits, displayed where we can all see them. I put up an attractive background paper so that the portraits really stand out. The aspect of display is always very important: If I am asking the children to produce excellent work and haphazardly slap it up on the wall, then I am giving a mixed message. By paying attention to attractive display I am honoring the children's work and giving it the value it deserves.

As the first children finish their faces, I stop the class to discuss the characters that are coming to life around us. Who are they? What are they like? Where do they live? We make a list of all the things we want to know about the hotel staff: name, age, address, phone number, date of birth, occupation, family members, pets, hobbies, interests, sports, favorite food. This list becomes a biography form that the children fill out for their character. They write their biography, mount it on black paper, and put it beside the portrait. Here, again, the simple structure of filling out a biography can lead to a more detailed narrative about the employee or can be the basis for a dialogue between two employees. I can use the structure to teach different modes of writing or to help a child who may be reluctant to write at all. This is a character that the student cares about, and all I am asking him or her to do is to tell me more about that person.

The wall of employee photographs is impressive, and we sit down in front of them to be introduced. A student begins, saying, "This is James Watson. He's one of the lifeguards at The Aquarium Hotel. He lives at 3141 England Avenue. His phone number is 342-8745. He is twenty-three years old. He lives alone with his cat Aqua. He likes boating and fishing and camping. He collects stamps in his spare time. He is also a weight lifter, and that's why he has such big muscles. His favorite food is spaghetti."

We take time to ask questions of the employees as they are introduced and pretty soon the staff comes to life. What is a typical day like for your employee? What are some of the problems that he or she encounters? Are there any safety concerns that might need to be brought to management? Who are the staff members that you are closest to? Who are the ones that you would just as soon not be around? Why?

Episode 3 The Hotel Suites *(3 weeks)*

I have chosen to focus our study on the design technology aspects of the hotel topic so I move fairly quickly from the staff to the design of the guest rooms in the hotel. I ask the students, *"What different kinds of rooms would you have in a hotel?"*

A student answers, "Suites! I want there to be lots of suites!"

I build on the answer, asking them, "What kind of suites would you have in The Aquarium Hotel?"

The discussion that follows is animated and fast-paced. We end up with a list that includes a honeymoon suite, a family suite, a disabled suite, an aquarium suite, a business suite, and an economy suite.

Before choosing the suite that they want to design, we have a discussion about what makes a good group member. I write the ideas on a chart. They include things like listening to everyone's ideas, being willing to compromise, contributing your fair share, and not having to have your way all the time.

Then I tell them, "I want you to find three other people in the room that you think you can work with, and follow these guidelines that you have come up with. When you think you have a good group, please sit in a circle together facing each other." When the groups are all settled, I go through the list of qualities one item at a time, and ask each member of the group to say that they agree to do this to make the group work. It is actually a solemn time as the children look into the eyes of their group members and say each of the things. I explain that I now expect that the groups will work out most of their own problems based on their willingness to work together. This is taken very seriously.

"Now it's time to begin the design work on your suites!" I tell them.

The suites will eventually be made as scale models in cardboard boxes, but first they must be designed to scale on centimeter graph paper. This involves several math lessons on scale. We measure things in the room using unifix cubes. We draw an object in the room to scale, first on the overhead together and then individually on paper. Scale models of bedrooms are done for homework, and gradually the children begin to see how scale works. Lots of questions come up:

"How big can a suite be?"

"Must each suite be the same shape?"

"How many suites can there be on one floor of the hotel?"

"How many of the walls can have windows?"

These questions arise naturally out of the work because they must be answered in order to build the models. By the time each group has finished their scale drawings a week has gone by. The groups share their drawings with one another, and modifications are made where necessary. All during the week there is spontaneous sharing going on as one group makes a discovery and shares it with another. This sharing happens freely. Anyone who has information that could be useful to the process is anxious to give it to all.

Once again, children spontaneously bring in outside resources to help. Someone has gone to the library and brings in a book on blueprints. One of the mothers in the class is an architect, and she comes in to share some ideas. A father who is an engineer sends in some working plans for us to look at.

When our plans have been shared and approved, each group brings in a box to start building its model. Ideas fly around the room as each group makes different discoveries. One group brings in doll furniture from home and uses it for the furniture in their suite. Another group spends hours making hand drawn wallpaper to cover the walls. Someone discovers a way to make a realistic toilet using a pop-bottle cap, cardboard, and Scotch tape. Walls are made within the rooms using smaller pieces of cardboard cut out with an X-Acto knife. A carpet remnant is brought in by a group and cut to size to make an elegant rug in the bedroom. A mom sews little draperies to be hung in the windows of one of the suites.

The sharing of these ideas happens in different ways. Some happen casually while the children work. At other times I stop the class to highlight the work of one group if I think that their idea is one that everyone will benefit from. Although I plan for two hours a day to work on the models, the work goes on throughout the day. Children come to school early and bring in things that they have made at home. Some kids ask to stay in at recess and others bring notes from home giving them permission to stay after school to work.

Sometimes I am called upon to act as a mediator when groups are having communication problems, or when someone in the group isn't pulling his or her weight. I am cautious about taking on this role. As the groups have made a commitment to work together, I make sure that the problem truly needs my intervention before I get involved. Usually this means that I interview the group to make sure that each member feels there is a problem and that the group has tried to solve the problem on their own first. We usually come up with an idea to try, and then we set a time to get back together to evaluate and see if the idea has worked. Because the work is motivating and they really care about it, the children are most often successful at working things out.

I also use my time to assess children's work. I take anecdotal records, gather scale drawings for a portfolio, and take a writing sample from a journal as evidence of a particular skill being used. The activities taking place in the room all require the application of the skills I want the children to learn. My only decision is what to formally document. The principle of the teacher's rope is clearly at work here. My curriculum goals involve the design technology work and the work with scale. But the children have a need to design and build suites and I have the tools for them to do that. They need to learn the skills to accomplish a task they care about. You can see why the Storyline topic must be so carefully planned. There must be a compelling reason to learn the curriculum provided through the logic of the story.

The classroom looks transformed. The hotel facade fills the back wall. Staff portraits and biographies fill the side wall. Charts are hung everywhere, one on top of the other. Scale drawings have taken over the blackboard. As the models are completed they are displayed on tables and bookcases around the room. I have each group write up a description of their suite that is taped to the side of the box so that anyone who walks into the room can appreciate what they are seeing.

When a group finishes well ahead of the others, they go on to solve any number of problems associated with the hotel. I ask the group to fig-

Figure 4–2. Box model of the honeymoon suite

ure out what they think needs to be done. We also have a class discussion to make a list of things we want accomplished, and groups sign up to tackle the jobs they are most interested in. No one is ever really finished because there is always work to be done to keep the hotel in operation. After a while the children stop asking me what they should do next. They just look around and figure out something that needs to be done.

We prepare formal presentations to share the suites with the class. Every group member is required to participate. When the sharing takes place we give specific feedback about the suite itself as well as the presentation.

Episode 4 The Customers *(1 week)*

Again, I question the students. "We now have a beautiful hotel, fully furnished with a top-notch staff to run it. What is missing now?" Several answer quickly.

"Customers!"

"Guests!"

"We need to have people come to our hotel."

Once again I build on this new stage of our project, asking them, "Well, *who do you think would come to The Aquarium Hotel?*"

Another class brainstorm list is created, and we end up with a long list of types of people who might want to use our hotel: businesspeople, celebrities, royalty, sports stars, musicians, families, foreigners, and politicians. This time we make small, full-body figures to create the customers. A simple structure for constructing a figure, using rectangles of cloth, bits of paper, sequins, yarn, foil, and so forth, is quickly given, and the children choose a guest that they want to make. Children with similar interests end up making the same kind of guests. New groups are formed naturally. The customers take about three two-hour sessions to complete.

When the guests are finished, the children work on writing a physical description. This is a very difficult task because they must try and tell only what can be observed about the character. I have the children focus on the actual features of the hotel customer that they have just created in order to give a good physical description. I give them a structure to clarify what I am asking for: Sarah Fitzgerald is about five-feet, three-inches tall. She weighs around one hundred and fifteen pounds. She has black hair and it is in lots of tiny braids. She has green eyes. Her nose turns up a little bit. She is fairly slender and she wears heels so she looks taller than she really is. She is African. She is wearing a long red dress with a black belt at the waist and silver buttons up the front. She has on blue shiny earrings.

This takes quite a while, and often during the process I have to stop and ask the children to look at their writing and check to make sure that they are only writing observable things. The actual figure before them helps to make the task more concrete, but it is still a challenge. This is a great opportunity for the children to develop their descriptive writing—one of the writing goals I have for this Storyline topic.

The finished hotel guests are mounted on black paper so they stand out, and then I take the physical descriptions, written on three-by-five cards, and shuffle them up. As I randomly read the cards out loud, the children must guess which character is being described. It's fun to try and figure out which character is being described based solely on a piece of writing. If a student's writing does not do what he or she intended it to do, then no one will be able to figure out who the character is. Here is a good example of an assessment tool naturally built into the topic. Children can quickly see if they wrote an effective description.

Episode 5 The Incidents *(2 weeks)*

With all of the physical elements of the Storyline in place, I ask the class, "All of the features of our hotel are in place and we are ready to open, *what do you think could happen in our hotel now that we are open for business?*" The replies come quickly:

"There could be a fire!"

"Someone could get stuck in the elevator."

"Someone could get food poisoning in the restaurant."

"There could be a robbery!"

"The washing machine could break down so none of the sheets could get washed."

Children piggyback ideas off one another and soon we have a great list of ideas. They go home on this day filled with ideas of what might happen at The Aquarium Hotel. That night, before I go home, I put some red, yellow, and orange tissue paper in one of the windows of the hotel, and use charcoal to make some thick black smoke. I am careful to not actually damage the work the children have done so I make sure that my fire can be repaired. The teacher's rope that I have carefully planned calls for the children to learn some of the health goals related to safety. The logic of the story has provided a natural opportunity to explore the issue of safety. The first child in the door the next morning is horrified.

"Oh no! The Aquarium is on fire!" she shouts.

As other kids arrive for the day, there is disbelief and shock. The class quickly goes to the frieze and puts out the fire, careful to restore the hotel to its original splendor. There is a loud buzz in the room as kids talk about what has happened and share horror stories of other fires that they have experienced, heard about, or seen.

"As you can see there was a terrible fire in The Aquarium Hotel last night," I say to them. "Fortunately, no one was hurt, but it is clear that we were not adequately prepared to handle this kind of emergency. We have to go to P.E. right now, but when we get back I would like to call a staff meeting of all hotel personnel so that we can discuss what to do to avoid something like this happening again."

The children are excited as they head for P.E. When we get back we go straight to the rug to discuss the fire. I begin by saying, "Each of you has a different task to perform at the hotel and I am sure that you may have noticed certain conditions around the hotel that are not as safe as they could be. *What do you think we could do to prepare ourselves in the event of another fire, and how will we respond if a fire should break out again?*"

There is a heated discussion about the conditions in the hotel. Children refer to their box models, the frieze of the hotel facade, their customers, and the staff. I begin to make a list of all of the concerns that are raised, and pretty soon we have categorized these concerns into a few specific areas where we need to make some changes. Task forces are formed, and various staff members sign up to work on the task force that interests him or her. Some children work on designing a fire escape plan for every suite in the hotel. Some figure out a way to add a sprinkler system to the ceilings. One group makes signs to place in each suite to tell what to do in the event of a fire. A group decides that there are too many plantings too close to the building and they set out to change the landscaping so that the hotel is less vulnerable. There is also a discussion of whether or not to make our hotel a nonsmoking facility.

When the groups are finished, they present their work to the class, and we debate whether we have adequately addressed the problem. Places are found to display the new work and children write in their journals to articulate the work we have done to make The Aquarium Hotel safer.

Meanwhile, I have chosen six of the incidents from the list the children generated of what might happen in the hotel. I pick things that will give the children a variety of experiences to explore. Speaking to the entire class, I tell them, "Now that we have been able to work as a whole class to solve a problem at the hotel, I want you to work in smaller groups to look at what else might happen at the hotel. I have divided you into groups of four, and I want each group to pick an incident out of the hat. Whatever you get, that is the incident I want you to work on."

After the children have chosen an incident, I explain that I want them to act out that incident and then figure out a solution for it. They are to put together a skit in which they can be either their staff member or their guest at the hotel. The skit needs to involve everyone in the group. We discuss as a class what we think would make a good skit. The list looks like this:

- Everyone must be able to be heard.
- Each member of the group must participate.
- You have to use some props, costumes, and scenery.
- The skit can't be longer than fifteen minutes.
- You have to show a realistic solution to the problem.
- The skit must have a script, written by the group.
- The script must be neat and readable.

Each of these ideas is given a one-point value. This criteria will be used when the skits are presented to determine a score or grade. The highest score would be a seven.

I ask the children if they think that there should be a minimum score for a group to pass. Surprisingly, the children say that no one should be allowed to get lower than a six. They say that a group that gets less than a six should go to study hall to work on their skit until it has a six or higher, and then present it again to the class.

The work on the skits goes on for about a week. Some of the groups end up doing research to help them figure out how to respond to the incident. The group working on a theft at the hotel calls a policeman to find out what he would recommend so that the hotel will be safer in the future. The school cafeteria staff is consulted on the incident involving food poisoning. Some of the research involves books. Movies, tapes, and filmstrips are ordered from the audio-visual catalog.

As in previous activities, I act as a facilitator. When a group has a particularly good idea, I stop the class to let them share it. A parent of a child in one group is talented at making costumes, so I check to see if that parent can work with other groups as well. We are operating as a community of learners, and as such we take advantage of all the talents available to us. The class understands that our collective knowledge is a real asset. They see firsthand the value of cooperation and collaboration.

If groups find that they are taking longer than they expected to complete their skits, we negotiate for more time. There is always the option of taking work home or staying in at study hall to work.

The class next to ours has also created a hotel, and the noise involved in producing the skits has spilled over. "Can we see their skits too?" the students ask.

I arrange with the other teacher, my deputy head, for our classes to be together for the skits. Having a bigger audience makes the skits even more flamboyant. Together, the classes help to critique each other's skits, each according to their own criteria.

Episode 6 The Visit *(1 week)*

After the skits are over, I tell the children that I have arranged for a guest to come and visit our classroom. The manager of The George Hotel downtown is coming and is very interested in seeing our plans for The Aquarium Hotel. I explain that they will have the chance to share their work with him and then ask him questions about his hotel. Then I ask students, *"How will we prepare for the visit of the manager of The George Hotel?"*

Everyone is excited. We all know The George, which has been a hotel since medieval times, and it is amazing to think that the manager would be interested in our hotel design. The children prepare for the day by planning out their presentation, deciding who will speak and about what, and also making up a list of questions to ask.

My conversation with the hotel manager on the phone is very amusing. First, he has never been asked to come to an elementary school before. Second, he is used to preparing a presentation, not coming to a presentation and answering questions. He is enthusiastic but cautious.

The day of the visit arrives, and the manager is greeted at the classroom door and given a seat of honor at the front of the class. The children have carefully orchestrated the whole event so I stay in the background as much as possible. My job is to videotape the event so that we can watch it later on and take it home to share it with parents. The manager of The George is with us for an hour and a half. He is genuinely impressed with the design of The Aquarium Hotel. He asks the children questions about specific things he notices. Sometimes they have a ready answer and sometimes they realize that they haven't considered something very important. The question time is intense. The manager is surprised at the depth of questions he is being asked. The children are honest and frank. Everyone is thoroughly involved. They really care about how their hotel relates to real-world hotels.

Some of the things that the children discover aren't to their liking. They think that their ideas are better. In other cases, the hotel manager gives them ideas that they want to incorporate into their hotel. In the end, the manager passes out flyers and a coupon to the hotel restaurant. The children are thrilled. He tells them that they have come up with some very good ideas and that he plans to take some of them back and share them with his staff.

When the visit is over, we discuss how we think it went and write thank-you letters. The staff portraits and guests are taken home, and the groups decide who gets to keep the suite model. The head teacher is so impressed with the facade of The Aquarium Hotel that she asks us to move it out into the central hallway of the school where it remains until the end of the school year.

I look back on the work we have done and am impressed by the scope of what the children have learned. I have samples of student work that demonstrates their competence in the key curriculum issues of math, design technology, health, and language arts. The children have had the chance to reflect on what they have learned and to share that with a professional. I know that the learning will last because it took place within a context that was created by the children. Their pride of ownership was evident when they shared their hotel with the manager of The George.

5 *Space Adventure: Operation DSCV*

This Storyline topic had a new challenge. I had not yet tackled one that would involve children working in the same groups for most of the duration of the Storyline. Irvington School has a racially and socioeconomically diverse student population, and I found that getting children to work cooperatively in groups toward a common goal was a persistent problem. I wanted to see if the context of a meaningful Storyline and the anticipation of taking a simulated space voyage would motivate the children to work together in a new, more productive way. Cooperation and teamwork were major goals for this Storyline. I was intrigued by the idea that the children would be designing a complete life support system and then actually testing that system out. I wondered if I would be able to keep quiet and allow the children to experiment on their own and learn from their mistakes.

Because the story involved space travel and colonization of another planet, I also had some science, social studies, and health goals. I wanted the children to figure out what a person would need to stay healthy in a completely artificial environment. I also was interested in having the children look at some of the social studies issues involved in traveling to a new home.

I began by asking the students, *Why do people move, migrate, or explore?* Lots of hands shot up, and we quickly got a wide variety of ideas: to explore new territory, to escape persecution, to build a new life, to get away from too many people, to be able to live in freedom. By the time we were finished, the list covered two pieces of chart paper. I never cease to be amazed when I seriously listen to the ideas of my children; their collective knowledge usually surpasses my own personal knowledge on any given subject. This had not always been my experience, but over the years my work with the Storyline method has convinced me otherwise. I have the highest respect for children's thinking.

Then I asked them, *What groups of people or individuals throughout history have moved, migrated, or explored?* This question elicited an amazingly eclectic list, including African slaves, Marco Polo, Christopher Columbus, Eskimos, Native Americans, Europeans, and even Ibn Buttuta! I had each child choose one of these individuals or groups to concentrate on and assigned them the homework task of trying to discover why these people had moved, migrated, or explored. The following day each child reported back to the class, and we put up a list of all the reasons. We discovered that the reasons people moved, migrated, or explored were pretty much the same no matter where or when they lived:

- People moved because of a shortage or a natural disaster.
- People migrated because they were being persecuted and they wanted the freedom of a place where they could live in peace.
- People explored because they were looking for riches or for the challenge of conquering the unknown.

It was a revelation to the children to see that there were so few reasons for people to move, migrate, or explore. These questions and the discussion that followed set the stage for the letter that we received the following Friday. (I had written this letter on behalf of NASA, knowing that I would send the children's recommendations to NASA with a teacher who would be attending a Teacher In Space conference.)

> Dear Students,
>
> We have been informed that your fifth-grade class has been seriously studying mathematics and science this year. We are also aware of your ability to stay on task, cooperate, and listen. You seem to be mature, responsible students who are capable of a special mission. NASA would like to invite you to design the inside of a space vehicle that will be used to transport others to colonize another planet. NASA will supply the plans for the exterior of the Deep Space Colonization Vehicle—DSCV—but the interior design will be up to you. We recommend that you build a prototype of your design and try it out for a day so that you can see how well it works.
>
> Should you accept this offer, we would like you to prepare a final report that outlines your data and findings and includes your recommendations for the real DSCV. NASA values the input of children in this important project.
>
> Sincerely,
> NASA Space Vehicles Engineering Department

The excitement in the room was palpable. *What should we do?* the children asked. We prepared a Costs/Benefits list to help us look at all of the issues that would affect our decision.

Costs	Benefits
We might have to use a lot of class time.	We could learn about space.
Something could go wrong.	We could learn about architecture.
It might be scary.	We might help colonize another planet.
We could get hurt.	We are working with NASA.
	We MIGHT be FAMOUS.

I felt a bit of panic rise up in me as I asked the children to put down their heads and vote whether or not to accept the challenge NASA had given us. Fortunately, a large majority of the children voted yes. What would I have done for the next three months if they had said no?

I learned a lesson at this point in the Storyline that I have never forgotten: Be careful that you ask the right key question. Whatever information the children come up with must be valued and used in the topic. If you ask the wrong question you are stuck with the wrong information, and you may have to go in a different direction than you had planned. I had asked the wrong question: How should we respond to this letter? It seemed like the right question at first, but I failed to consider all of the possible responses, one of which could be that we should not accept the challenge! In actuality, that possibility was brought up by some of the children who felt that if we spent all of the time necessary to carry out this project we would get behind in our schoolwork and not finish the fifth-grade curriculum! Others were concerned that this was too dangerous a project, and they didn't want to take the risk. On the other side of the discussion were the children who felt that it was a real honor to be asked to participate in this project. They felt that we were being given the chance of a lifetime. Luckily it all turned out the way I hoped it would.

In order to begin the work of designing the interior of the DSCV we needed to answer the key question, *What do people need to survive?* After all, the people traveling in our vehicle to another planet would need to survive for quite some time in space. The list the children generated was as follows:

food and water	oxygen	heat/air conditioning
correct air pressure	clothes	a place to sleep
a bathroom	light	scientific equipment
medical supplies	first aid	exercise equipment
airtight hatch	escape pod	refrigerator
emergency supplies	ropes/cables	radio/radar
map/compass	lounge room	a computer/printer
a way to keep clean	rocket power	a tool kit
windows	flag	fan
fire equipment	storage	a kitchen
backup systems	gas gauge	artificial horizon

From this list we decided that we needed to categorize these things so that we could form work crews to make sure that all of these needs were met. I picked an item from the list at random and put a red star by it. The children then told me all of the other items on the list that could go together with that item and I put a red star by those as well. This process was repeated until we had five colors of stars that corresponded to five groups of items. The children gave names to each of these groups, which became the focus of our work crews. They were:

Food
Light and Oxygen
Emergencies
Bodily Needs
Scientific Equipment

As I mentioned earlier, one of my primary goals with this Storyline was to provide opportunities for my children to learn the importance of cooperation and teamwork, so I did not let the children choose their own groups. I knew that these groups would be together for a long time, and their success would be dependent on a good mix of children within each group. I spent a good hour creating five groups that contained a variety of abilities as well as groups that had a workable mix of children from a social standpoint. The following day I told each child which group they would be in, and the groups began to work.

In the past, I would have thought ahead about what the children would need to conduct their research and I would have gone to the library and gotten a good selection of books so that when the children asked for material I could give it to them. A good teacher anticipates the children's needs and has resources available to meet those needs; however, my previous experience with the Storyline method led me to believe that the children would figure out a way to get the information they needed. The principle of ownership was clear at this point: The children felt such a strong sense of purpose that I trusted that they would not hesitate to ask for help when they needed it.

After our first work session, several groups came to me and said that they had no idea what to design for their system of the DSCV because they didn't know anything about what a space vehicle should look like. Because they were designing this for NASA, they wanted to be sure that they designed something that was similar to things NASA had used before. We had a discussion as a class, and everybody agreed that they wanted to go to the school library the next day to see what information they could find there. I checked with the librarian, and she arranged an extra time for us to come down and check out books related to space.

The initial excitement of the children as they found books about space was very short-lived. They took the books eagerly back to the class, and each group began to pore over the contents. Pretty soon several kids came up to me with comments like, "These are stupid books. They don't have any of the right information." "These books were written for little kids and they don't have any of the stuff that we need." "None of these books have enough information to do us any good."

Where do you think we could get the information we need? I asked. Almost immediately one of the children suggested the downtown public library. "I've been there before with my mom, and it's huge, and they have tons more books."

That's a good idea, I said, but how are we all going to get to the public library? Will they let a whole class of kids come at the same time?

"Couldn't we call them and see if we could come and then decide?" They were persistent.

I answered, Sure, but what will you say when they answer the phone? Who do you want to talk to and what will you ask them?

At the end of this lively discussion I had a group of three children who agreed to write a script for what they would say to the librarian, and I gave them a pass to go to the office and call. Meanwhile, the other groups were drawing, sketching, and discussing their ideas for the various systems they would eventually design for the DSCV.

After several minutes, the children returned from the office. "They said we could come and they will even have some extra librarians there to help us if we give them enough warning. They want you to call them and tell them the date and the time we are going to come."

Wow. How exciting for the class to discover this newfound power! They could actually figure out a way to get information, and they could plan a way to acquire it. How are we going to get to the library?" I asked. There was a period of silence. No one had thought of that.

"Couldn't we just order a school bus?" one hopeful child responded.

We could, I said, but that would cost quite a lot of money, and we don't have any money for buses right now.

"What about taking the city bus? I have a bus pass." There was a low murmur around the room as a few other children said they had passes too. "You can buy books of tickets at Safeway and that makes it cheaper."

That's a great idea, I said. I would be happy to buy the tickets if you bring me the money. I also think we need to let the bus company know that we are coming. We are a lot of bodies all getting on the bus at once.

In the end, a group of children agreed to call the bus company to let them know when we would be coming, and the group that called the library called back to tell them the time we would be arriving and how long we would be staying. This was the first time a class of mine had initiated the idea for a field trip and planned the whole thing. I was pleased to see that the motivation of wanting to know more about something they cared about had produced such results. I decided that because the kids were so focused I didn't need to ask for any parent volunteers to go along. We knew why we were going, and I was convinced that we would have no discipline problems on the trip. The children wrote up the permission slips, and in a week twenty-six children and I were headed to the bus stop to go downtown to the library.

When we got off the bus we had a few blocks to walk, and I reminded the kids of the need to stay close to me and to watch what they were doing. This was unnecessary teacher worrying: The kids were so excited about the prospect of getting information on their DSCV project that they weren't misbehaving. The context of the Storyline provided all the children with a clear focus. They had determined the need for this trip and they knew what they hoped to accomplish.

At the children's section of the library I let each group sit around one of the library's computers to begin a search for the information they needed. When they found the title of a book that looked promising, I told them to write down the call number and then take it to one of the librarians who could help them find it. There were three extra librarians on duty, which made it much easier. Soon after we arrived it became clear that many of the books the children wanted to look at were in the adult stacks on the second floor. I told them that if they could justify to me why they had to have one of these books for the system they were designing, then I would take them up to the adult stacks in groups of three. I cleared this with the five librarians in the children's library. They were impressed with the focus of the kids and were happy to stay with the rest of the class while I was upstairs. Never before would I have thought I could leave my whole class in the hands of strangers in downtown Portland while I went off looking for books! This is the power of the Storyline method.

We were at the library for just over an hour, and I was exhausted at the end of the time, but we had several new books to take back with us and the children were thrilled. The books were fairly advanced, and most of the things in them were way over the kids' heads, but they had great pictures and a few good diagrams. They felt like they knew enough to start making their various life support systems for the DSCV. Because there was a purpose for these books, the children were not deterred by the advanced language. They were happy to use what they could, and were able to zero in on the information that was useful to them and not worry about the rest.

The group work, once we got back to school, was far more involved and complicated than I had thought it would be. Many of the groups had difficulty listening to each other. The work itself was challenging. It was tough for the kids to visualize what this space bubble was going to look like, and consequently how much room they had to design their various systems.

We called a class meeting, and I suggested that we go to the Science Lab where the bubble would be erected and measure off the space so we could make a scale model on graph paper. We paced off the dimensions of the lab and decided we wanted to make our bubble as large as we could within that space. Using a scale of a square inch to a square foot, the groups drew diagrams of the equipment they were designing and brought them up to put on the model which was up on the front blackboard. This visual became a very important part of the process: When every group had finished putting up all of their equipment, we realized that there was no room left in the bubble for the people who were traveling! Many groups refined their designs and decided that stacking things on top of each other was a very good idea! The group that was designing the sleeping quarters decided that the beds would be recessed, vertically, into the walls since gravity wasn't a problem.

To help us visualize the space we first had to determine the total square footage of the floor of the bubble. Then we divided that figure by the number of people who would be spending the day in the bubble. It was amazing to all of us how little room we had to live in. Our study of area in math took on new meaning.

This process of designing and building the systems for life support took almost five weeks. Each group struggled with its own particular set of problems, and we often had to meet as a whole class to decide what to do about them. One problem in particular became of great importance to the whole class. It was brought up by the Bodily Needs group: How do you pee in space?

Naturally, the children wanted to know how they were going to go to the bathroom during their whole day inside the space bubble. They quickly rejected my idea of just letting people go to the bathroom down the hall if they really needed to go. "You can't just go out into space and pee, Mr. Creswell. Things stay out there forever. Gross! You don't think they just open the airtight hatch and let you out every time you have to take a leak, do you?" they asked.

Well, I replied, this is a simulation and I don't think NASA would really care if we adjusted that part. Dead silence and ugly stares.

Over the next two weeks we spent a great deal of time trying to solve the problem of elimination in space. The children saw two basic problems to overcome:

1. How do astronauts deal with the problem of weightlessness?
2. How do they dispose of the waste once they have used the bathroom?

One of the boys in the group suggested that they could use Ziplock bags. He reasoned that they were lightweight and could contain the waste after you were through. The girls in the group were not at all sure that this was a good idea. The problem was that none of them was eager to try it out. This was not a problem for the boys, who went straight to the bathroom to prove to themselves how easy it was. The girls in the group started to ask other girls in the room if anyone was willing to try out a Ziplock bag, so that the group could proceed with their plans. In the end, only one girl in the class was willing. The two girls in the Bodily Needs group asked if they could go along with her and stay in the stalls on either side so that she could report the progress of the experiment to them. She was glad to have the company. Although the other groups were working on their systems during this time, I could tell that everyone was anxiously awaiting the return of the threesome from the bathroom.

"It was easy and I didn't even get anything on my hands!" shouted the jubilant guinea pig as she returned from her mission. The class spontaneously cheered and she was congratulated and slapped on the back by her peers.

This process went on until the final bathroom was completed. By this time, the Bodily Needs group had surveyed every class member to see how many bags they would need for our day in space. Everyone had kept track of the times they used the bathroom during one week in school. This figure was divided by five to determine a daily average. With class list in hand, the members of the Bodily Needs group called out everyone's name and each student reported the number of bags he or she would need. By this point the group had discovered another innovation: sponges were placed in each Ziplock bag to absorb the liquid and make the sealing of the bags easier.

The bags were placed outside the bathroom—a large refrigerator box painted black with a door carved in the front and a hole in the back with a black plastic garbage bag taped over it. If a person needed to use the bathroom, he or she took a bag and went in after turning over the sign to indicate "The bathroom is in use." There was a chair to sit on and next to it a spray bottle of bleach and water and a carton of baby wipes. After using the Ziplock bag, the person would seal it and stick it through the hole into the garbage sack. Next, bleach and water were sprayed onto the hands to disinfect them. The bleach was washed off with the baby wipes.

This whole process was very difficult for me to let happen. My teacher voice kept whispering to me that I was treading on shaky ground! Yet I believed in the power of the process and I trusted that the context of the Storyline and the ownership the children felt would keep

Figure 5–1. The famous bathroom from the DSCV

everything in perspective. I never had a single worried phone call from a parent, and the kids didn't really talk about this to any of their friends. It was viewed as one of the many aspects of the larger project they were working on.

Every group had its own problems to tackle, and by the time we were a week away from liftoff we were panicked that we wouldn't be ready in time. The next key question put them over the top: *How will we celebrate our liftoff?* The children asked me if we couldn't spend all day working on the mission. I said that I was concerned about the other work I had planned for the week, but if they were willing to do that for homework, I would let them work all day. No one squawked, and so extra homework was given and we were able to have everything finished by the Friday of our liftoff ceremony.

The groups that finished their systems first worked with me on making the actual bubble. We made it as large as the science room and tall enough that the ceiling would be over eight feet in the middle. A visit to the nearest high school to talk to a physics teacher who had made a bubble with his students proved very helpful. We assembled it by duct taping it to the floor of the classroom and setting a large box fan by an open window with a tube of plastic connecting it to the bubble.

Once we had turned on the fan and inflated the bubble, we slit the side next to the classroom door and inserted our airtight hatch. This was an ingenious design using a dishwasher box and two doors made of clear plastic, sealed with Velcro. All of the systems the children had designed were brought in through the hatch and set in place the night before our liftoff. The walls of the bubble were surprisingly rigid when it was inflated, and we hung up our daily timetable, our exercise routine, and our list of jobs to use during our day in space.

These charts were the result of several class meetings when we answered the key question, *How will we spend our day in space?* We discussed what we were going to do all day in the bubble, how we would use the exercise station, and what jobs everyone would perform. It was a very difficult thing for the children to imagine how a space traveler might spend a whole day in space. The discussions we had forced the kids to consider this thoughtfully because they knew that whatever they planned they would have to live with for the entire day of the simulation. As a teacher I loved the fact that this natural consequence made the children take the process very seriously. They paid attention and worked together because they saw a real reason to. Unlike a traditional lesson on cooperative learning, the Storyline provided a context that demanded cooperation.

The big day arrived. The liftoff ceremony included a short speech by our captain and the singing of "This Land Is Your Land." The two other

Figure 5–2. The DSCV airtight hatch

fifth-grade classes and several parents were present for the ceremony, and they formed a tunnel down the hallway as we walked down to the bubble and all crawled through the airtight hatch. The Emergencies group had written a script for the liftoff procedures. A local cellular phone company had lent us two sets of phones so one of the other fifth-grade classes acted as ground control for us. Everyone held their breath for the countdown protocol and suddenly we were airborne! The children took their roles and referred to the daily itinerary they had designed.

Each student had a large Ziplock bag with their lunch in it, which had been prepared by the Food group. This included such innovations as dried fruits and vegetables that they had dried in class and boxed juices, which they knew wouldn't spill in a weightless environment.

There was an exercise center that everyone used in shifts, which included an exercise bike with special straps to keep a weightless person from floating off and provide resistance. Each child had a journal, and the events of the day were recorded and reflected upon at designated times throughout the day.

During the morning we had the excitement of a visit from a reporter and a photographer from the local newspaper who stayed for almost two hours. In the afternoon, our second-grade buddies visited us, and we shared our spaceship with them. During each visit the children proudly shared the various systems of our space bubble and answered questions.

It was very stuffy and hot inside the bubble, even though we were drawing our air from the outside. We were all in shorts and T-shirts and wished the Food group had thought to bring jugs of water in addition to the boxed juices. Sweet fruit juice did not do a great job of quenching thirst. Many kids wrote in their journals to remind themselves to tell NASA that lots of fresh water was important to take along!

The bathroom sat inconspicuously in a corner of the bubble, where it was used throughout the day without any particular notice from anyone. One child wrote in his journal: "I learned from the bathroom that it is not embarrassing. Nobody makes fun of you as you use the bathroom. It was kind of fun to use. I went to the bathroom and some other people went to the bathroom. We all decided to do it so we did it. The bathroom was a black cardboard box. It had a sign that said, 'I'm Using the Bathroom,' and everyone honored the sign and didn't make fun of you."

We were amazed at how quickly the day passed, and there were groans when it came time to land and we were again being guided back to earth by ground control on the cellular phones. Some children asked if we couldn't go again on Monday!

When we came back to school the next week, it was time to write to NASA. *What recommendations do we want to share with NASA?* I asked. The kids assembled all of their work in a topic book that told the story of our mission and what they had learned in the process. Every child took great pride in producing his or her own hand-bound book filled with drawings, lists, journal entries, the newspaper article, our mission patch, and some reflective writing on the experience. A representative sampling of these books were given to a teacher going to the Teacher In Space conference, and she shared them with the people from NASA at the conference.

As teamwork was a major curriculum goal for this Storyline topic, I had the children do a reflective piece of writing on what they learned about teamwork. What follows are pieces that came from two different students' topic books. One of these students is an average student. The other student is a special-needs child who goes to a resource room twice a day. When children are actively engaged in a meaningful project that requires the solving of real-life problems, cooperation, and commitment, it's hard to tell the difference.

What I think teamwork is: working together, being able to work with a variety of people. Even if one person in your group can't get along with a friend, your whole group could fall apart. You've got to know when to joke and when to be serious or you've got a big problem. If we were in a real spaceship and we didn't get along, we could have died. That is what I think teamwork is.

To me, teamwork means things you do with your friends. You get more done when you are in a team. It is a lot of fun to work in a team. I was happy when people agreed with me. A team is people that listen to each other. It is OK to not agree with people and to discuss it. I was on the "Food Group." Our team had troubles. We just decided to work together. We got a lot done when we agreed with each other.

6 *The Radio Station*

The Radio Station Storyline was the second I did with this particular group of children. I had moved down from teaching fifth grade to teaching a third- and fourth-grade mixed-age classroom. The following year I moved up with this class to a fourth- and fifth-grade mixed-age. The last two Storyline topics covered in this book were also done with this group of children in my second year with them. As you will see, these kids made some amazing changes in that time. They became a very close-knit community, and their academic growth was quite remarkable.

The Radio Station had a language arts focus. I wanted the children to learn about writing for a specific purpose, and I wanted them to learn to edit their writing for a performance that needed to be a specific length of time. I wanted them to improve their skills of observation through drawing and I wanted them to learn about the criteria used in developing a logo. There were minor goals in career education and in science.

We began the Storyline by reading this letter:

KBPS Radio
The Radio Station of Portland Public Schools

Wednesday, November 2, 1994

Dear Students of Irvington School,

Have you ever wondered what it would be like to build and run a radio station? We at KBPS, the radio station of Portland Public Schools, are looking for students who would like to create a radio station. We feel that our programming often doesn't meet the specific needs of the many neighborhoods where our schools are located.

Here is where you come in. If you would like to design and build a radio station for your neighborhood, we would be interested in hearing some of your programming and perhaps using it at our station. We are always looking for ways to involve children in our programming.

If you do produce a radio show we would like to have you send us a tape so that we could consider it for broadcasting. In return, we would like to invite you to take a tour of our station and see how we operate. Your work will help us to reach more students and involve them in radio.

Should you decide to take us up on this offer, please take the time to write and tell us so that we can make plans for your visit. We look forward to hearing from you.

Sincerely,
KBPS Radio Station

What is a radio station? I asked the class. This was a topic they all felt they were experts on. We made a brainstorm list that was two pages in length. There was no question that we would take up this offer from KBPS. This is a sample of one of the letters the children wrote to the station telling them that they would like to design a radio station for their neighborhood:

Dear KBPS,

I like this idea about building a radio station. We will be building our station on Broadway. I am truly thankful because you liked us and we would like to build a radio station.

Sincerely,
Juan

I knew that this would be a high interest topic. I had talked to the manager of the station prior to writing this letter, and she was enthusiastic about supporting our study. She said they had a program that was geared for children and they would certainly be able to broadcast some of the children's programming.

Where should we build our radio station? I asked. "I have chosen a five-block area on Broadway that I think might have some empty storefronts and also some empty lots. We need to decide whether we want to design our own building on an empty lot or whether we want to use an existing storefront. This afternoon we'll walk around the area and see if we can find something that will work. I'd like everyone to take clipboards so that if we do find something we can begin to sketch it. We are going to use the sketches to help us build a frieze of the station in our classroom. We'll then build a model of the station in our classroom and set up our recording studio."

It was a warm fall day when we set off for the main drag in our neighborhood, a few blocks away from the school. I had chosen the location because it was in easy walking distance from the school, and I wanted us to be able to walk there several times to look at the chosen site and to make sketches as necessary. It didn't take long for the children to choose a site they loved. Broadway is an area of rapid growth, with lots of new shops and businesses moving in. An old movie theatre had recently been renovated and turned into three storefronts: a burger joint, a pizzeria, and a New Age boutique that had just folded. They loved the new exterior, but what sold them was the fact that they could see a bathroom in the back of the store through the front window. It was the spot! We crossed the street and sat on the curb and began sketching the building. They decided that our frieze should be the whole building because it would be too difficult to just isolate our radio station space. Each child had several pencils and a few pieces of white drawing paper. I explained to them the importance of signing and dating every sketch so that they could keep everything in their working portfolios for later use.

"Look, Mr. Creswell, they have the number of the company that's renting the place on that sign and the name of the person to call. We need to write it down so we can find out how much it's going to cost." Adam was sure that building the station here on Broadway was a distinct possibility, and he wasn't going to stop until he figured out a way.

Remember, I told them, we don't have to worry about such practical matters because we will have our model in the classroom to work with. I tried to get him to accept our limitations, but once he had suggested the possibility everyone thought it was terrific. I smiled that day after school when I was looking at the sketches and saw that most of them had the name of the real estate agent and his phone number in the corner.

The next day in class we determined the space we would use on our back board, and the kids divided up the task of making the frieze into logical work crews: windows and doors, the building itself, awning, signs, and landscaping.

Adam wanted to know if he could go and call the real estate agent. Apparently, he was not content to let the idea die. Adam is a student who finds writing torture because it means he has to sit still for too long to do it. I said that he had to write out a script for the phone call before I would let him go down to the office. I hoped that this would put him off, but by the end of the day he handed me a script he had written with a few other kids, so I said that they could call the next day.

We began building the storefront the next day, and after the first ten minutes, Adam was back from the office with the news that the agent was out of his office, but he had left a message and he would be calling back later in the day. Sure enough, that afternoon the office called to say that there was a real estate agent on the phone asking for Adam. We all waited on the rug while Adam went to the office to take the call. We could tell by his face as he came back into the room that it wasn't good news.

"He was really nice and he was glad that I called, but we will never be able to afford the building. It costs three thousand dollars a month to rent," Adam said.

There was a long silence in the room before a little girl raised her hand and said, "My grandmother likes to bake cookies. Maybe we could have a bake sale."

The discussion that followed left the children feeling hopeless about the prospects of finding the money to actually rent the space. My attempts to remind them that we were building a model in the classroom and could do everything we needed with the model were not met with enthusiasm. I had to just move along in the creation of the frieze and hope that the kids would throw themselves into that process and forget about the high cost of starting a small business. Fortunately, after a few days the money worries were left behind in the enthusiasm for constructing our frieze.

The groups soon realized that the sketches they had done did not have enough detail and they wanted to go back to the building to do more sketches of the specific part of the building that they were responsible for. We were lucky that the weather was cooperating so we took off to do some more sketches. Some kids needed to be close up and others needed to be a distance away, so I took a parent along to help me supervise.

It was fascinating to watch the kids head right to their area and begin to work on their sketches. They needed to know specific information and they were eager to get that information so they could continue their work on the frieze. The desire to create an accurate model had given them a reason to want to know more, and they had framed their own questions as they discovered all that they *did* know and realized all that they *did not* know. What are the frames around the windows made of? What do the door handles look like? Are the booths in the hamburger place black-and-white-checked? Are those decorations on the walls painted on, or are they tiles? How is the awning attached to the building? These sketches were very specific, and many of the children wrote in the names of colors so that they would know what color of paper to use when they got back to the classroom. They were very focused as they worked, and there was a lot of consultation between group members as they checked with each other to make sure that they drew everything they needed to.

Back in the classroom the groups went right to work with their newfound information. The awning group struggled with how to show depth on an awning. The perspective was difficult, and everything they tried was unsuccessful. Finally, someone suggested that they make the awning 3-D. It was the perfect solution. The real awning ran the length of the building and rose in an arc over each of the doors. It was anchored to the building with steel rods. They used one long strip of white butcher paper for the awning and they accordion-folded it to get the corrugated effect. This was anchored to the board with strips of white construction paper, which were just strong enough to hold the awning at a ninety-degree angle. It was an impressive solution to the problem, and everyone in the group gained new status because of it.

The process of building the frieze is a very messy one. I am definitely not in charge. My role is that of facilitator. I ask questions, make suggestions, and supply materials when asked. At the end of most work sessions I also act as a reflective agent, helping the children to express what they think has worked well that day and what they feel they need to work on the following day. In the beginning of the process the children work exclusively in their own work crews, but as things progress it is not unusual for some kids to move to help another group that needs an extra hand. Sometimes this move is facilitated by me, but more often the children arrange it themselves as they notice that one group is finished with a task and another needs more help. The collective ownership of the frieze increases as the image comes to life in the classroom. Standards set by the children are extremely high, and they will work and rework until they get it right. This is clearly a process that comes from the children themselves because of their high degree of ownership.

The frieze took about three weeks to complete, and when we were done we had a beautiful storefront to put our radio station into. The next key question I asked them was *What should we call our radio station?* The list of ideas was terrific: KASS (Kids Are So Smart), KIDS (Kids Radio), KPIC (Kids Put In Charge), KASC (Kids Are So Cool), KAPT (Kids Are People Too), and KCRS (Kids Choice Radio Station). After a discussion and a vote we became KPIC (Kids Put In Charge).

One student's father owned an advertising agency. He agreed to come in and talk to the kids about designing logos. He brought in photocopies of all of the logos of every radio station in Portland. He explained that a logo needed to be simple and eye-catching, that it must work well close up as well as far away, and that the name of the station must stand out. He made a big point about the use of color. "If you are going to use color in a logo you need to be prepared to spend three times as much money. You also need to make sure that your logo will work as well in black-and-white as it does in color, because there will be places you want to use the logo that only use black-and-white."

From these suggestions, we compiled a list of criteria for our radio station logos. Then the children were turned loose to design a logo for KPIC. I gave them the choice of working in pairs or working alone; I didn't want anyone to feel left out of the process because of his or her

Figure 6–1. Frieze of KPIC with staff portraits above

artistic ability. We worked for three days on logos, and in the end we had about fifteen to choose from. Now came the difficult task of picking the one logo that would be used for KPIC.

I decided that we needed to review the logo criteria before voting for the logo we would use. Not surprisingly, the two finalists were the only logos that had decided to use color. I told the kids that before we took a final vote, I would have to make a copy of each logo so that we could see if they worked as well in black-and-white. I didn't get to make the copies until after school that day. As I suspected, neither one of the logos worked in black-and-white. One of them had been done with special felt markers that produced a subtle blend of colors. These all turned to a muddy grey on the photocopy, and the letters KPIC were not clear. The other logo had used yellow for spotlights pointing to a sculpture of the KPIC call letters. It was striking in color, but in black-and-white the yellow turned to a muddy grey that obscured the letters.

I felt trapped. I wanted to somehow rescue these kids from the disappointment of thinking they were the finalists to realizing that their design failed one of the key criteria. I knew that it would be very hard for these particular students to accept defeat. I also knew that I owed it to all my students to follow through with the criteria we had decided upon.

The next day I put the copies up next to all of the other logos and let the kids see for themselves; I didn't have to say anything. The children said at once that we needed to take another vote. It was difficult. The two children who thought they were finalists were really upset. I let them have some space and suggested that I make copies of all of the logos and then we could vote again.

The two former finalists asked me if they could try again and redo their logos. I thought about it and then said that it wouldn't be fair; everyone had known the criteria from the beginning, just as they had, and they had chosen to risk using color. If I let them redo their logos, then, in fairness, I would have to let everyone redo their logos and we didn't have time for that. They stayed upset.

The next day we looked at all of the logos, discussed their merits, and voted again. A logo that had received very few votes the first time around ended up being the winner. For this bright but socially isolated child, it was the high point of his year. He was amazed at the newfound status he had in the class. He suddenly felt that his peers respected his talents.

The following day a parent, who is a computer consultant, volunteered to take the logo and scan it so that we could have logos in different sizes to use in our radio station. I saw this as the perfect opportunity to bring the three potential winners together. I asked them if they would like to work with this parent on the computer, learning how to use the scanner and making copies of our logo. All three of them jumped at the chance, and the experience of working together erased the anger and replaced it with the excitement of using the technology. As they each came back to class beaming, with a page full of logos, it was clear that the larger context of the Storyline had taken over, and these kids were again involved in bringing KPIC to life. It was a good lesson, which they never would have learned had I chosen to rescue them.

What do we need to know before we start to produce our radio show? I asked. By this time in the Storyline, the children were full of questions. We made a chart, and from there we divided into work crews to find out the answers.

1. What are we going to use for equipment?
2. How are we going to advertise?
3. How do we get a frequency to broadcast?
4. Where will we put our logo?
5. Will we need to make changes to the building?

6. Where will we get money to pay our bills?
7. What will our station look like through our front window?
8. Who is going to actually broadcast?
9. How big does a sound studio need to be?
10. What does a sound studio have in it?

Some of the groups set off to do research while others began working on parts of the radio station itself. One group wrote a letter to the FCC requesting information on how to apply for a broadcast frequency. Another group worked on designing the equipment for our sound studio. A group worked on the storefront window on our frieze. One group began to look into Thomas Edison and the invention of the radio, and the last group researched the process of sound waves being converted to radio waves. Each group ended up with a different product that showed what they had learned. At the end of this two-week process we made a list of all of the things we found out. We were all impressed by the knowledge we had gained.

THINGS WE FOUND OUT

1. AM radio waves have different lengths.
2. FM radio waves are closer and further apart.
3. We need recording equipment.
4. Kilohertz equals 1000 cycles per second. Megahertz equals 1,000,000 cycles per second.
5. We need a control board, transmitter, microphone, transmitting antennae, and a soundproof room.
6. Thomas Edison invented the radio.
7. Radio is regulated by the FCC, the Federal Communications Commission. The FCC issues frequencies and call numbers.
8. Sound waves have to be changed to radio waves in order to broadcast.
9. All call numbers east of the Mississippi begin with "W" and all call numbers west of the Mississippi begin with "K."

Now that our radio station was up and running, the logical key question became *Who works at KPIC?* From a long list of possibilities we ended up with the following list. I decided that if we had a day shift and a night shift, then we would have enough jobs for everyone in the classroom. The jobs were as follows:

secretary	disc jockey	weather person
manager	producer	assistant manager
station owner	janitor	security guard
studio manager	advertising director	control-board operator

The children first created a 3-D portrait of the person they wanted to be at the radio station. These were framed and hung on the board above the radio station facade. Rather than write a biography of the character, each child filled out a job application for their person, telling about themselves and listing their first three choices of jobs at KPIC. Here is Juan's application for his character:

> **Name:** Tony Suarez
>
> **Age:** 20
>
> **Ethnic Background:** Spanish
>
> **Address:** 1435 7th Street
>
> **Phone Number:** 331-0917
>
> **Family Members:** Wife, age 19; brother, age 16; son, age 2
>
> **Hobbies or Interests:** Basketball
>
> **What jobs do you want at KPIC?** Security guard or janitor
>
> **Why do you feel you are qualified for these jobs?** Because I used to work in a hospital as a janitor. That's why I want to be a janitor. And I work in a bank as a security guard and they said I work good.

After everyone had finished their job applications, we began the long process of hiring people for the various positions. I had a list of all of the jobs on a chart and a stack of Post-it Notes. After reading the job application out loud, we could put the character's name on a Post-it Note and place it next to the job of their first choice. If, in the end, we had more than two people for the same job, we needed to go back and read the job applications to determine who were the two people most qualified for the job.

This was an interesting lesson in the importance of good writing, because it became clear to the children which applications presented the characters in the best light. If we had a question about an application we would ask the person who had made the character to respond, and the child, in role, would answer the question. The life of our radio station was so real to us that it seemed natural that we would refer to each other in character whenever we were working on KPIC.

It took almost three hours over two days' time to finally figure out the staff for KPIC. This was intense time, and the whole class actively engaged in the discussion that often turned into a heated debate as the children tried to explain why their character was uniquely qualified for the job of choice.

The staff was eager to develop our programs as soon as they were all hired, so we started with the key question *What programs will we broadcast?* Here are the initial program ideas:

movie theme songs	comedy	rap
children's writing	radio drama	news
community calendar	Motown music	reggae
game shows		

One of my goals for this Storyline was for the children to improve their writing skills, so I asked them to develop a script and work within a strict time parameter. I developed the following criteria, which would help give children a handle on the specific things they needed to do to be ready to broadcast. These became central to the process of developing the programs—we were constantly referring to them when kids got stuck or frustrated.

Criteria for Radio Programs

Each of these criteria is worth one point. Your program must meet all of these criteria in order for you to go on the air.

1. Your program must be no longer than three minutes.
2. You have to speak clearly.
3. Your program should be interesting and educational.
4. Everyone in the group must speak during the program.
5. Every program must have some music that is performed by the group.
6. Each program must have a typed script.

I wanted a high level of participation on these programs so I decided that groups of three would design them. Each group got to choose what program they wanted to produce. We worked for three weeks on the programs. It was a very chaotic and often frustrating time. The children found it very difficult to be specific in their scripts. They left out many things and had to go back and add things in that were so obvious to them but not to someone reading the script cold. We had many class meetings where each group would share what they had so far, and the class would give them feedback according to the criteria. We also timed each program, and many groups had to go back to the drawing board to add more to their program. The kids were astounded at how long three minutes was when they were having to plan it so carefully. Some groups ended up with programs much shorter than three minutes and other groups borrowed time from these groups because they knew their show would be over time. In the end we had the following shows produced by the radio station staff whose names appear below. This was our master list, which we wrote on Post-it Notes so that we could move things around easily, finding an order that would work best. This was the order we finally came up with and used:

KPIC Program Guide

1. Oldies (4 minutes): George, Jeanah, and Emily
2. Comedy (1 minute, 12 seconds): Josh, Matt, and Serena
3. Radio Drama (1 minute, 30 seconds): Ebonisha, Jessy, and Gina
4. Science Tips for Rainy Days (1 minute, 15 seconds): Jamie, Katey, and Jazzminn
5. Motown Music (2 minutes, 7 seconds): Antonio, Emily, and Peter
6. News (2 minutes, 23 seconds): Sarah, Tony, and John
7. Children's Writing (1 minute, 23 seconds): Marshe, Lamarianna, and Andrea
8. Rap (4 minutes, 3 seconds): Zo, Andre, and Deion.

We arranged with the music teacher to borrow her recording equipment for a day, and when the time arrived we pushed back the desks, put a "Do Not Disturb" sign on the classroom door, and began recording our programs. It was a half-day process, and I was astounded at the ability of the children to stay focused and disciplined throughout the recording session. We had to do many, many takes before we got each show the way we wanted it. The patience of each group and the willingness of the children to go back and do things over were exemplary. We were all part of a team, and we knew that we had to all do our best if the final product was going to be any good. In the end we had a radio broadcast that lasted about twenty minutes. It was the most concentrated twenty minutes that any of us had ever experienced!

Now that our tape was made we were ready to take it to KBPS and see what a real radio station looked like. *How do you think our radio station will compare to the real thing?* became the next key question. I called the station manager and let her know that we were ready to come. She arranged to have one of the student disc jockeys interview our students about KPIC in one of the sound studios. Our school was within walking distance of the station, so we took off about an hour before our scheduled tour. I had our tape in my pocket. It seemed funny to think that this little bit of plastic and magnetic tape represented the culmination of three months of intensive study. It was a typical winter day in Portland, with a few breaks in the clouds followed by light sprinklings of rain. On our way the conversation was filled with anticipation. The children had all kinds of predictions as to what a real radio station would be like and how it would differ from our own station.

KBPS is largely run by high school students, so my kids were completely enthralled from the moment we walked in the door. This was the real thing, and it was run by kids not much older than themselves. We were met at the door by the station manager, who said how glad she was that we had taken her up on her offer to create our own radio station. We toured several sound studios, the music library, and the editing booths; in every place there were high school students at work. My students asked many questions: "Don't you get tired of planning all the shows?" "What do you do if you can't think of anything to say?" "Do you have to record things over and over again until you get them right?" "How do you keep track of all the buttons in this sound booth?" "Has anyone ever made a big mistake when they were on the air?" "Do you ever start laughing when you are on the air because you're nervous?"

The high school kids were blown away by the level of interest and the quality of the questions they were asked. It was obvious that these children saw themselves as insiders in the world of radio.

After the tour we were led to a large sound studio where the afternoon DJ recorded an interview with the class about the creation of KPIC. We recorded the interview in pieces, going back to make sure that everything was clear. It took us probably twenty minutes to record a five-minute interview. After it was over, we eagerly walked back to school knowing that the interview would air that afternoon at 2:00. The energy on the walk back was palpable. Kids were comparing and contrasting KBPS and KPIC. There were several conversations going on at once, each dealing with the visit and what had been learned. I was able to walk from group to group and listen to all of the ideas flowing freely through the class. I was impressed.

Back in the classroom, the radio was plugged in, and we had trouble getting anything else done before 2:00. Five minutes before the big moment we gathered on the rug around the radio. I was reminded of those scenes in the old World War II movies of anxious families gathered around the radio listening to Churchill announcing the end of the war. The DJ announced our interview and there was a collective gasp of excitement from the class. We laughed. We groaned. We relived every moment we had back in the station during the taping. We understood the magic of radio as well as a whole lot more.

Our Radio Station topic was officially over at this point, but we spent the next three weeks putting together a topic book that documented the whole study. I had asked the children to go back to the beginning and tell me what we had done step-by-step. I asked, *What should we put in the book to document each step of the process?* Here is the table of contents that they came up with:

1. The letter from KBPS
2. Our letter back to KBPS
3. Chart of the possible names for our station
4. Sketches of our building
5. Color photocopy of our frieze
6. Journal entry about finding our building
7. My logo design
8. Our official logo
9. KPIC questions to answer in our research
10. List of things we found out
11. Report from my work crew
12. List of who works in a radio station
13. My job application
14. Criteria for radio programs
15. Our program ideas
16. Order of our programs and times
17. Journal entry on the trip to KBPS
18. What I learned from our KPIC study

Making these books allowed each student to summarize, draw conclusions, and analyze what was learned. They became a valuable tool as well as a treasured remembrance of the KPIC Storyline. I found them invaluable as an assessment tool when it came time to document what the children had learned. They were the cornerstone of our spring student-led conferences, and parents reported that they were amazed at the depth of knowledge and the enthusiasm that had come out of the KPIC study.

I was satisfied because all of my goals had been met and I was confident that the children had learned these goals in a way that would not be forgotten. The experience of creating a radio station had given meaning and purpose to the curriculum.

7 *The Huk-Toocht Fish Farm*

We sat on the rug, and the anticipation was tangible: this was the start of our first Storyline topic of the year. This class had been with me the year before, and I had moved up with them to teach a fourth- and fifth-grade mixed-age. I was interested in seeing how the children would respond to a second year of working with Storyline topics. My major areas of focus in this topic were science and social studies. We were going to study the ecology and the politics involved in the issue of dwindling salmon in the Pacific Northwest. I also wanted to accomplish goals in art, language arts, and research, which became the minors.

I told the children that we would be building a town on the Oregon coast called Huk-Toocht. Huk-Toocht means "good luck" in the language of the Chinook Indians.

The questions started flying. "Do we get to decide what Huk-Toocht looks like?" "Can we draw pictures and share them with everybody?" "How much room do we have to build the town?" The experience of this class from the year before was evident. They already were anticipating how the story would unfold. This confirmed my belief that the Storyline method provides children with a template for learning. I stopped the questions to read the first extract. In some Storyline topics an extract is read to give children some specific information that they will need to create the story. In this case I was setting the stage for Huk-Toocht, a town on the Oregon coast where we were going to design and build our fish farm. Once they had this information, they could let their imaginations blossom.

HUK-TOOCHT

At first sight, Huk-Toocht is like many other townships on the Oregon coast. The scattered farms and homesteads surrounding the blue-green bay edged by barbed wire fences look toward the mouth of the Wauna

> River and the Pacific Ocean beyond. Inland, behind the town, the misty mountains of the Coast Range rise dramatically against the often grey skies. The rural community of Huk-Toocht has some special characteristics that are to its advantage. Being on the Coast Highway 101, it is quite accessible and, in recent years, people from the metropolitan areas of the state have found it an attractive place to settle down. Some of them, like Roderick Cameron, came to escape the pressures of city life and worked hard at farming. Most local people are farmers first and foremost. They have a small amount of land on which to grow hops, berries, and cranberries, or to take a crop of hay. In the stonier and wetter land away from the coast they graze sheep or keep a small herd of dairy cows. Such land is insufficient to support a family, so most farmers have other occupations. With ready access to the sea, most have boats and fish supplements the food that can be produced on the land. Others are employed as part-time shopkeepers, postmen, builders, or weavers. In summer, during the tourist season, some local people take on additional jobs; some become drivers, others guides, while others open their homes to guests.
>
> Huk-Toocht can be reached by car without too much difficulty. The county highway winds along the Wauna River with passing lanes on most of the steep grades. Traffic is seldom heavy, although during the short summer tourist season it is much busier. Most members of the community would not like to see traffic get any heavier.

What do you think Huk-Toocht should look like? I ask the class. We read the extract several times, and from it the children created a list of important features to include in the frieze. In groups of four the children went off with big pieces of paper to design the town and to share their designs with the rest of the class. We worked for a few hours, and the next day groups took turns sharing their ideas. We kept a chart of the best parts of each design. This process was a long and sometimes arduous one, but the skills of visualization, design, and cooperative planning that the children were learning more than justified the time. I was pleased to see them using the knowledge and skills that they had acquired during our Radio Station Storyline from the year before. At the end of the session we had six different "Best Parts" lists, and we looked at these, circling the features that appeared on more than one list. We also cross-referenced the list of features with the information from the extract. This gave us a list of features that would be included in our classroom frieze of the town. I suggested six different work groups: background, animals, transportation, landscaping, farms and houses, businesses and town buildings. The children chose the group they wanted to work in, and the groups went off to design their pieces for the frieze.

Because I had worked with these children the year before I knew that they had the skills necessary to choose good working groups. We had spent a lot of time discussing group work and practicing the skills of cooperation so necessary for this to be successful. The previous year I had taken the time to carefully plan my work groups, making sure that I had a good mix of children from the standpoint of ability, social skills, gender, and ethnicity. All this preparation paid off. I was now confident that our community of learners knew each other well enough to make appropriate choices. After all, one of the things that makes the Storyline method powerful is its way of bringing together kids to work cooperatively on a task.

I worked with the background group because the scale they chose would affect what was built by all the other groups. Since the other groups were just drawing preliminary designs, I wanted to get something up quickly so that when they were ready to start building they would have a sense of scale. Children want their work to look good, and one of the roles of the teacher is to facilitate that by providing the children with structures that help them achieve the goal or standard they want to attain. Some of the background group worked on the ocean using tissue paper strips and starch on a white background to produce the depth and range of colors seen in the sea. When the tissue is applied to the white paper with starch, the colors bleed and swirl together creating an ocean-like effect. The other half of the group worked on creating the sky by sponge painting with three good Oregon sky colors: light grey, dark grey, and pale blue. Both the sky and the ocean were done on large, two-foot-by-three-foot panels, and then hung across the width of the board we were working on. After these were up, one group went to work making the Wauna River, using a mosaic of different watery colors of painted papers, randomly cut into ovals of varying size. The rest of the group made the coast range of mountains by layering painted papers that had been torn to show the ragged mountain tops. When torn toward the painted side, the white edge makes a distinctive contour. The background of dark green fadeless paper below the mountains and above the sea was now ready for the rest of the groups to begin putting up their creations.

Meanwhile, the other groups were figuring out how to make trees, animals, houses, fences, cars, roads, signs, and all the other aspects of the town. Frustration was high but so was creativity. Everyone wanted their contribution to be of the highest quality; pieces of work went back to the drawing board several times before they were considered finished. Again, structures were provided to help the children manifest their ideas. One suggestion that made a big difference was to outline all the details on the buildings in black. This made the features of the buildings stand out and allowed for the addition of small details, such as doorknobs and windowpanes, branches and individual leaves. Everything on the frieze was put up with sticky tack so that things could be moved around and changed as needed.

As a finishing touch, I put a black frame around the whole thing, which set it off as elegantly as if it was on display in an art gallery. A day did not go by without someone fussing with something on the frieze, to move a building, change a sign, add an animal, or build a road. The individual tasks of the groups faded at the end, and everyone pitched in to finish what needed to be done. The town was ours in the true sense of the word.

The frieze, as it took shape, transformed our classroom. Parents, other students, and visitors were spontaneously brought in to see the results. People were awestruck by the beauty of the town we created, and our enthusiasm for the process was contagious. I was pleased to see that this frieze showed many signs of improvement over the one we had made for the KPIC radio station. I could see that the children were applying their knowledge and experience from the year before.

Writing about our town was a natural extension of creating Huk-Toocht. The best writing comes from something we know well and care about. Our town was truly a rich source of inspiration that we wanted to tap. I started the process by having the children brainstorm lists of words that captured the frieze for them. We began with nouns, then moved on

Figure 7–1. Frieze of Huk-Toocht

to verbs, adjectives, and adverbs. Each of the words was put on a three-by-five card. I gave the word to the child who had called it out, and he or she would take a bit of sticky tack and put the word on the frieze where he or she thought appropriate. The words almost covered up the artwork, which brought howls of protest from the children! I resisted taking them down for a few days because I wanted them to see the range of possible words that they could use when writing about the town. Eventually, I had the children put the word cards in pockets on either side of the frieze labeled with the appropriate part of speech. This process allowed each child to test his or her understanding of the parts of speech as the decision was made where to put each word.

Then, I asked the children to use words to describe what they had created artistically. I challenged each child to make their writing so strong and clear that without looking at the frieze I would have a vivid picture of our town. It took several writing periods for everyone to produce a finished piece. I was pleased to see the word cards being used in this process as the children looked for words they wanted to spell or just to get ideas for the right word to say what they had in mind. The writing the children produced was remarkable. No one had to hunt for inspiration because the frieze was right before our eyes. Everyone had an intimate knowledge of this and it was reflected in the finished pieces.

> Huk-Toocht means "good luck." I think it sounds like gathering up spit and spitting it out doesn't it? We started Huk-Toocht with just some plain old green paper, but soon it looked like a masterpiece. The dirt roads were in, the farms were all done. The buildings in Huk-Toocht looked great. The animals were spectacular and the background was great. There was a beautiful river called the Wauna River. It led into the ocean with its light blue, dark green, and dark blue water. The ocean was flowing; well it looked like it was. You could actually tell where the woods were without a word bank card! Mr. Creswell told us about Huk-Toocht and even he was surprised. The clock was covered with red cellophane to look like the sun. I thought that was a good idea.

> A nice town with the ocean in front and the mountains in back. You can see the mouth of the Wauna River and the river itself as it flows through the middle of the town. The sky is usually powdered with clouds and is overcast. The houses are scattered with the farms, stores, and schools. Huk-Toocht has many colors including green, blue, red, yellow. . . . That's all for now!

The children were ready to move on to the next episode of the topic: we would make the families who live in Huk-Toocht. I wanted the children to explore a variety of different families, so I gave them the surnames for six different families and the occupations for two of the adults in the families.

1. The Stewarts: a farmer/postal worker and the post office manager
2. The Larsons: a handy person and the hotel cook
3. The Washingtons: a fisher and a weaver
4. The Martinezes: a veterinarian and a teacher
5. The Franklins: a children's author/tourist boat operator and an artist/potter/owner of the craft shop
6. The Camerons: a retired contractor and the hotel manager

What will the families of Huk-Toocht be like? I asked the children. It was up to the groups to decide what each family was like and to create all of the family members. One of the families, the Camerons, had a husband named Roddy, who was to be the main character in the story. The whole class helped to make him. Whereas the other townspeople were small paper figures, Roddy was made full size with a 3-D portrait head and clothes that were brought from home.

Once again, I encouraged them to choose their own groups. They knew that they would have the chance to work on their own and to work in a variety of groups throughout the topic. I gave the children a structure for making a little person. They were given a piece of paper that was eight inches tall and told that this paper represented the height of a six-foot-tall adult. When the paper was folded in half, the children could see that half of the paper was three feet. When the top and bottom halves were folded into thirds, the children then had markings for every foot to guide them in producing a character that was of the proper height and in scale with the other members of their family.

The children knew how to make these people from the year before, so the work they now produced was much more sophisticated. Each group was given a large piece of colored tagboard to mount their family on. Next to their character they put the biography, which they wrote after completing the figure. With a fat black marker, I wrote each family's name in the middle of the tagboard so that it could be clearly read from the display. All of the families were put up on either side of the frieze. Again, the characters were mounted with sticky tack so that as they were introduced or we needed them for an episode, we could take them down and move them around. It was at this point that I read the second extract.

Roddy Cameron

Roderick Cameron, or Roddy, as he prefers to be called, came to Huk-Toocht from California in 1975. He had been a house builder in Los Angeles, but became tired of urban life and, because of his great love of the open air, decided to set off for the Oregon Coast to make a new beginning. When he saw Huk-Toocht, he knew immediately that it was the kind of community where he could settle down. In 1978, he met and married the minister's daughter, who taught in the two-teacher school, and they have two children.

Roddy is now a farmer, having had to learn the hard way how to cultivate the coastal land, which, although sandy, sometimes yields stones that can wreck a plough, and to shear the hardy black-faced sheep of their wool. Since he had been a builder, it was relatively easy to supplement his income by taking on odd jobs for people in Huk-Toocht or, occasionally, for the Huk-Toocht Town Council or nearby hotels.

Roddy was the resident of Huk-Toocht who was going to start the fish farm. The first children to finish their own characters worked on making Roddy and dressing him with clothes that were brought from home. These were attached to the board with push pins and folded and bent to look realistic.

It was time now to meet the people of Huk-Toocht. The introduction of the characters was great fun. Everyone had a story to tell, and the relationships between the people of Huk-Toocht naturally evolved as we shared. At one point we even had a budding romance start between children from two of the families! This fertile mix of imagination and prior knowledge kept the story alive and hence the children's anticipation. Everyone was always waiting to see what new incident would happen next.

The next extract introduced the children to a problem that Roddy needed to solve.

Roddy's Problem

Fishing was the love of his life, and once or twice a week he went out in the bay in his little boat with his two dogs. He was usually able to bring back enough snapper, sea bass, or salmon, according to the time of year, to provide for an evening meal for the family. Yet he knew full well, as did others like him in Huk-Toocht, that it was often a matter of luck whether you found the fish or not. What would be so much better was to farm the fish just as people long ago had learned to farm animals on land to provide a reliable source of food. He had read a lot about fish

> farming experiments and realized what was involved. So, what he really wanted to try was fish farming.
>
> Roddy leaned upon the front gate of his farm, which looked toward the sheltered waters of the Wauna River. He wondered how he could realize his ambition. This occupation would combine a lifelong hobby with a new source of income. He sighed. What he needed was money, and that was something he lacked.

We discussed the situation as a class. *What would Roddy need to know if he were going to start a fish farm?* I asked. It was clear that we needed to get some information to help him make up his mind. I knew that at this point in the Storyline it would be ideal to go out into the field and find out more about fish farming, I had planned a field trip to a local fish hatchery on the Columbia River and to an Interpretive Center that was in the Columbia River Gorge, a national scenic area just outside of Portland. The trip was more than just a day spent away from school. I told the kids about the purpose of the trip, and everyone was eager to find out all they could. Once again, the teacher's rope is a critical element in planning a successful Storyline topic. I needed to know ahead of time when it would be logical to go on the trip, and I had to make sure that everything was planned ahead of time. Yet, even with my prior planning, the children still owned our town and the people in it, and they felt that they were creating the story as we went along.

My teaming partner made up a scavenger hunt for the children to use on the field trip. This contained questions that the children had raised concerning the raising of salmon, such as: "What would it cost to purchase fingerlings from a hatchery?", "What kind of salmon grow in Oregon?", and "What sort of food do you feed salmon?". Each child took their "Research for Roddy" along with a clipboard and a pencil so that they were well prepared to jot down all that they found out.

As both our classes had made their own version of Huk-Toocht, it made sense for them to go on the trip together. It was interesting to see at one point when we were getting ahead of the other class in the construction of the frieze that my children suggested that we spend an afternoon helping them get caught up. We did just that, and the two classes worked happily together as my children were able to share their knowledge from previous Storyline work with a group that was less experienced. The sharing community we had built in our classroom naturally extended to peers when there was a need.

The clear purpose for the trip made it a great success. Each child brought back his or her scavenger hunt resource sheet, and it became the first piece of resource material to use as we studied the business of fish farming. We had a wonderful class discussion as we debriefed the field trip and talked through all of the information we collected. Everything we learned was put on a class chart so that we could use it later.

Coincidentally, our local newspaper, *The Oregonian*, came out with a special section on salmon in the Northwest, so we had that as a resource as well. At this point I wanted the children to do some in-depth research into the issues surrounding salmon. A newsletter to educate people about the problems that salmon were having in our part of the country seemed an ideal way to present the information that the children discovered. The newsletter could be used by Roddy to share with people about why he was starting his new venture.

What do people need to know about the salmon situation in the Northwest? I asked next. The class was divided into five research groups to investigate various aspects. Again, these were different groups from those that had made the families. Salmon in the past, salmon in the future, financing and fingerlings, life cycle, and food and habitat were the study groups. Each group had the task of finding information and then writing an article for the newsletter, complete with original illustrations.

To provide a focus to the research we wrote a list of questions about what we wanted to know about salmon. We also wrote responses to the question *What is a fish and why is it of value to us?* The groups sat together, and their first task was to write down the questions from our chart that pertained to their area of research. Then each group member chose a question to answer. Books were checked out from the library, files were downloaded from the World Wide Web, and books and pamphlets were brought from home.

The financing and fingerling group decided that they needed to call the Oregon Department of Fish and Wildlife because they wanted to know where they could buy fingerlings for Roddy's fish farm and how much it would cost to buy food to feed them. They wrote out a script so they would know what to say and then they went to call accompanied by a parent volunteer. The parent later told me how amazed she was at the confidence that the children showed in their telephone conversation. They clearly knew why they were calling and the information they needed. The people they talked with were happy to help them, and a week or so later, they received a packet from Fish and Wildlife with several pamphlets, many of them with Post-it Notes explaining things in more detail. The group was quite excited with their newfound information. Their article for the newsletter could now begin to take shape.

Each group was also asked to create some illustrations for their article. A parent had volunteered to scan the children's drawings and insert them into the finished product. I agreed to type the final drafts so that they could be put into newsletter format on the computer. This was a very intense part of the topic, and several of the groups needed lots of individual attention. Our resource-room teachers, who assisted in the classroom, took one of the groups and led them step-by-step through the process because they weren't able to work independently. Parent volunteers came in to conference with writers, and every spare minute of my time was spent advising, typing, editing, or helping children to locate a new source of information. In the end, we got an amazing array of articles, diagrams, and drawings. We even created a fish farm coloring book for children, complete with word finds, crossword puzzles, and mazes. The published newsletter, professionally laid out on the computer, was a great source of community pride. Here is a sample article written by the life cycle group:

> HOMECOMING HAZARDS
>
> Close your eyes and imagine yourself an alevin. Imagine yourself growing up to be a fingerling. Now you are leaving the fresh water. You feel the cool water going through your gills as you go down the waterfall. Now you are in the channel flowing to the salty ocean. You are there! You feel proud. You see some food and you eat it. The sun is going down and you can't see it coming into the ocean anymore. You see covering rocks and you make your way in and lay there for awhile. Now you see sunlight coming back into the ocean. You get up. Ahhh! You see a shark. You are not far from where you rested. The shark is chasing you. Faster, faster you swim. You are there. You try to go back, but there is something inside. You see another hole. You squeeze inside. You are safe. The shark goes away, but you stay there. You are hungry, and you see something floating down. It seems to be stuck to a string. You grab it very quickly. As you tug on it you feel yourself being lifted up. You spit it out just in time. Different things happen to you, but you survive. You feel something in your mind telling you to go back to fresh water. So you go back, only because it is bothering you. You've started to go back. Now you stop because you are so tired. You relax for awhile, but you've got to keep moving! You see a dam. You keep going. Now you are there. You are hopping up. You keep going. Aha man! You are so tired. You stop and turn around and let the water run through your gills. You turn around and keep going. You are almost to the top of the fish ladder. Two more, one more, you are there! Now you're turning around so you can breathe. It feels so good. Uh-oh, now you remember. You swim to the place where you were born. Ah, you spawn. Now you have floated to the top of the fresh water and you are dead. You finally accomplished your mission. You have spawned and you will bring more salmon into the world.

Now that we knew all the issues about the salmon, the next task was to decide *Where should Roddy build his fish farm?* Each group was given the following guidelines and a map they used to choose an appropriate site for Roddy's fish farm. They then wrote a persuasive letter to the Oregon Department of Fish and Wildlife explaining why their site should be considered. One of my language arts goals was for the children to demonstrate their ability to write a persuasive letter. We had done a minilesson in writers' workshop on persuasive writing, and here was a logical place for them to apply what they had learned.

> CHOOSING THE SITE FOR THE FISH FARM
>
> You will have noticed that Roddy has spent a lot of time reading about what he had to do in setting up a fish farm. He could not just start a fish farm anywhere at sea. He knew he needed permission to locate it on an appropriate site. Although many parts of the coast of Oregon—including the coast around Huk-Toocht—are promising areas for setting up fish farms, there are many considerations to take into account. Roddy learned about these from the reports and documents he had read. Here are some of the considerations:
>
> 1. Fish farms ought to have good, deep water, be sheltered from storms, and be readily accessible by boat.
> 2. They should not be too near other fish farms or shellfish farms to avoid spreading disease.
> 3. On land there should be a suitable base with services, like electricity and water, and storage facilities should be easily reached by van or truck.
> 4. They ought not to be too near scenically attractive areas, nature reserves, or fishing grounds, and be clear, too, of harbors and channels used by boats.
> 5. Fish farms are not always attractive-looking so should be tucked out of sight whenever possible using natural screens of rocks or trees.
> 6. Waste (or effluent) from fish farms can cause pollution risks unless care is taken. Nets also have to be cleaned regularly to ensure a good water circulation in the cages.

Again, the groups were different because the task was different. I let the activity determine the grouping because I find that when there is a clearly defined reason for group work, the group usually functions more efficiently. The letters to Fish and Wildlife, along with the maps marked with the possible sites, were photocopied and placed in the children's working portfolios. These hanging files, alphabetized by last name, are in an easily accessible spot in the room. All of the work on the topic is dated and kept in this portfolio. At the conclusion of the topic, it will be assembled into a topic book, which will be an episode-by-episode record of the story of Huk-Toocht.

The letters were sent off, and within a week Roddy had received a reply. Although each group had chosen a different site, each of the groups had chosen a place that met the criteria, so the assumption was made that all of the sites would be accepted. A town meeting was called so that Roddy could read the letter of acceptance to the Huk-Toocht residents and share his plans for starting his fish farm. We decided to videotape the town meeting so that we could share it with the visitors at our grand opening celebration. Each student came to the town meeting dressed as their Huk-Toocht character. They each wore a name tag around their necks with their character's name on it so that they could use the correct name at the meeting. I was elected to read the part of Roddy. The parent who volunteered to do the videotaping filmed our life-sized Roddy while I was doing the talking for him. The children wanted me to understand that I was *only* Roddy's voice—nothing more! Here is a copy of the letter of acceptance that Roddy read:

THE OREGON DEPARTMENT
OF FISH AND WILDLIFE
SALEM, OREGON

Dear Mr. Cameron,
FISH FARMING PROPOSAL

I refer to your application for a seabed lease for the purposes of salmon farming at Huk-Toocht.

Following public advertisement and consultations with interested parties, the commissioners of the Oregon Department of Fish and Wildlife have decided that a lease should be granted for the required area as shown on the attached plan. The scale of development permitted in the leased area will be limited to the number of salmon cages stated in the application. To safeguard the landscape, dark matte gray color should be used in all the installations other than navigation markers.

This site has been found to be acceptable to all the other authorities, and is unlikely to have any significant effects on fishing, conservation, or recreation interests.

A lease will now be sent to you for your agreement as soon as possible.

This letter is being copied to persons who submitted comments on the application.

Yours Faithfully,
M.J. Gravestock
Oregon Department of Fish and Wildlife

It was fascinating to see the town of Huk-Toocht come to life as the citizens debated this new venture and its impact on their way of life. There was a lively discussion of the pros and cons of Roddy's fish farm. The following list was generated during the course of the meeting:

THE PROS AND CONS OF RODDY'S FISH FARM

PROS	CONS
1. Jobs	1. More rowdy people
2. Brings in money	2. Takes money away from others
3. Place to visit for the children	3. Ruins picnic places
4. Other places to swim	4. Dangerous to children
5. No serious harm to swimmers	5. Spoils countryside
6. More large fish	
7. Help most people	
8. Help babysitters	
9. Support Roddy	
10. More fish not less	

In the end the town voted, by a narrow margin, to support Roddy's new venture. I can honestly say that I had no idea what the result of the meeting would be. There were times when emotions were running high and I wondered if the town would run Roddy out on a rail. Although Roddy had clearly stated at the start of the meeting that he would start his fish farm regardless of the outcome of the meeting, I was relieved to see that the townspeople ended up on his side!

The next step was for the children to help Roddy design a fish cage for containing the salmon from the size of fingerlings to their adult size when they could be sold for food. *What would be the best design for a fish cage?* the students wondered. We knew about some of the problems associated with the design of such a cage because we had read aloud the book *Gentle Ben* by Walt Morey in which the family of the main character, Mark, had maintained a fish trap in Alaska similar to Roddy's fish cages.

The cages had to be anchored to the seafloor so they would not drift away. There had to be a way to feed the fish from some sort of a catwalk. There needed to be some kind of protection from predators who might see these fish as an easy meal.

Although read aloud was not a regular part of my Storyline time, I chose *Gentle Ben* because I knew that it would provide a natural tie-in with our fish farm topic. This is a good example of how the Storyline topic naturally becomes integrated into all aspects of the curriculum. Because the Storyline is a context created by the class and meaningful to them, they are constantly making connections in all areas of study.

We brainstormed a long list of considerations before we actually set out to design our cages. The children worked in pairs and began by doing a scale model drawing of their design on graph paper, which they had to have me approve. The models were then built in shoe boxes and displayed on a table in the room with their drawings and an explanation of how the cage worked. The boxes were turned on their sides with the top facing out. The side on top became the surface of the water and the inside of the box showed what was below the surface. The designs were very imaginative, and there was a lot of variety in the different approaches to the problem.

Finally Roddy was ready to open his fish farm. *How will we celebrate the opening of Roddy's fish farm?* I asked the students. The class decided that they wanted to invite their friends and families to the opening, so the following invitations were printed up and each child illustrated one to take home.

a special invitation

The Grand Opening
of the Huk-Toocht Fish Farm

Thursday, 14 December, 1995
3:30 to 4:30
Irvington School, Rooms 200 and 204

Highlights include:
a live musical performance,
videotape of town meeting,
fish farm newsletter

Light refreshments will be served

The children had to plan the whole event, and there was lots of talk about what should be included. In music, both classes had been working on composing background music to accompany the reading of some Native American poetry. They combined this with a Native American song they had learned and decided that they would open the fish farm with a joint performance done by both the classes that had worked on this Storyline topic. Every child had a part, either playing an instrument or doing a reading or singing. Next, they decided to have a ribbon-cutting ceremony. A bright red ribbon was strung across the table where the fish cages were displayed.

Our grand opening happened to fall the week before our winter break so we were able to order gingerbread dough from the cafeteria. The first part of that week we went down to the cafeteria and each child made a fishy gingerbread creation to serve as refreshments at the grand opening. We had salmon, octopuses, starfish, and eels—an amazing array! In addition to the gingerbread, kids brought in pieces of smoked salmon, with cream cheese and crackers to serve it on.

We displayed all of the charts we had created throughout the course of the Storyline topic. These were put up around the room in chronological order, so that parents and guests could be guided through the process we had gone through to start our fish farm. This was our opportunity to share all of the work we had done.

The grand opening was a brilliant success. We had lots of parents and supportive friends who came and enjoyed an hour of sharing, refreshments, and fun. I was pleased to stand back and watch the children proudly share our story. The children ran the whole show. It was impressive to listen in on their monologues describing each step of the process to their parents, retelling the whole story of how Roddy's fish farm had come to be. I had the luxury of sitting back and watching this event as it happened all around me.

Here's what Daniel had to say about the Grand Opening in his topic book:

> The Grand Opening was the best part of the study, at least to me. This is what I liked about it:
>
> - the ribbon cutting
> - the music
> - the refreshments
> - sharing stuff with my mom
>
> I think this was a very important part of our study and that's why I'm so glad that we did this and did so great! My favorite part of the Grand Opening was the music and the ribbon cutting because we did it perfectly, especially the music.

When the children came back from winter break they assembled their topic books. I was amazed to discover that the children were able to recall all of the details of the topic from the very beginning as we talked about what should go in the book. They came up with a list of twenty-eight different things that should be in the book in order to capture the richness of all that they had accomplished. In our discussion, one child said that she would like to send a copy of our Salmon Times newsletter to the Oregon Department of Fish and Wildlife. Another said that he wanted to send a copy to the local newspaper, *The Oregonian*. We decided that each child could send one copy of the newsletter to a person or organization of his or her choice. The children were so proud of the research they had done and they were anxious to share their ideas with a larger audience. Storyline aims to be a bridge to, or a mirror of, the real world. It is natural that children will make these connections when they have the chance to compare their own work with real issues in the world around them.

One of the pages in the book was a reflective piece of writing entitled "What I Learned From Our Study of Huk-Toocht." I did a brainstorm list with the class before they started writing and they filled four pages of chart paper with their thoughtful, enthusiastic responses.

Ashley wrote:

> I learned a lot about salmon and working together. Before we were picking our families I planned to be a little old lady who lived in a corner of the woods, widowed and all alone. As it turned out my person ended up being a sixteen-year-old named Rene Cameron. Everything turned out okay.
>
> Something of interest to me at the Bonneville Fish Hatchery was that they cut open the female's stomach and if her eggs fall out she is ready, but if they don't fall out she is not. Also, they put three females to one male and that a female digs a nest called a redd to lay her eggs. If another female digs a nest too close or on another female's redd, her eggs will die. I also learned that salmon have white spots when they die.
>
> I wonder if salmon have different personalities like humans?!
>
> One thing I learned for certain was that it takes a lot of imagination to build a town.

And Jonathan wrote:

> I learned why fish open their mouths when they swim in water. That's how they breathe. The water goes in their mouths and out their gills. I learned that salmon are like cannibals because they eat each other to stay alive. I also learned that it takes a whole community to get some-

> thing done. And did you know that female salmon have thousands of eggs? Or did you know that there are three kinds of salmon at Bonneville and they are Coho, Chinook, and Upriver Brights. And if salmon continue to decrease, in ten years there will be no more salmon. Some salmon migrate over 1,200 miles. Also, salmon have white spots when they die. And male salmon can spawn with more than two females. Only male salmon's noses hook at death. That's what I learned in the study of Huk-Toocht.

We experienced the story of Huk-Toocht as a community of learners, and our memories were a fertile mix of our own imagination and the facts we had sought out. The important processes and pieces of information that I, as a teacher, had wanted the children to learn were internalized because they were needed to make the story come alive. People do not remember disembodied facts. They remember experiences that they care about. We internalize the learning because we want to remember and savor the experience. In other words learning, to be memorable, must be meaningful.

8 *Underground to Canada*

A visitor to my classroom was talking to a young African American student at the beginning of our work on this Storyline topic. The student was explaining that this was going to be the best Storyline our class had done in its two years together. When the visitor asked her why this was so, she replied, "Because this one is about *my* people." My Storylines are always inhabited by characters who reflect the diversity of the students in the community where I teach. I hadn't ever stopped to think that my minority students might not feel the same sense of ownership that my European American students did. I had underestimated the validating power of studying one's own history. The following poem, written by Brenan in response to the escape of the protagonists of the story from a plantation in the Deep South, captures the depth of feeling and strength of conviction that this Storyline engendered in my students.

A strip of color,
A bit of imagination,
And a lot of courage
One dark night,
The north star
And a glimpse of ambition
You must have strength
To face the danger that lies ahead
Face to face
Confront it, and move on
The hounds will bay
Calling you back to chains
Resist
And pass it by
Sleep by day,
Travel by night

To reach your destination
You must have fate
The past is gone
So look to the future and press on
Follow the gourd, and cross to Canada
Keep your dream
Freedom
Till dawn is near, the hound will howl,
From losing your tracks in the water
Cross out danger,
Welcome hope, faith & love
A wolf or a bear would not keep you
Back
for if you put your mind to it, you can do it
Take a deep breath and press on till daybreak
Do not retreat,
do not repel,
Do not give up
Pass by all worries
For your load must be light
Follow your heart to the Promised Land
Be wise
Keep going
For when you get to your destination,
You will be free
Follow your dream
Freedom
All you have to do is
Follow the Drinking Gourd

This Storyline topic was based on the novel *Underground to Canada* by Barbara Smucker. I had never done a novel-based Storyline before this, and I had several questions about how it would work. First, I wondered where the ownership would come from since the story was already written in the form of the book. Second, I was curious about the children's ability to sustain interest over time with a topic so tied to history. Would they get bored and feel that the whole thing was predetermined and therefore lose interest? I was also puzzled by the issue of display: Storyline depends on the collective context, built by the children in the classroom, as the learning environment. Would the children accept characters they made from the book as their own? Would they be able to understand the setting, which would evolve very slowly through the course of the book? How would the visual display look in the classroom?

As with many of my Storylines, I was planning and implementing it with another teacher, my colleague and friend Rebecca Plaskitt. We took several days in the fall to write this Storyline and to think through the curriculum content that we wanted to emphasize. I was surprised to find that the planning took three times longer than any Storyline I had done before.

As a literature-based topic, we knew that we wanted the children to have lots of writing experiences. We also wanted to give them the opportunity to dig deeply into the literature and look at the author's style and the techniques she used to bring the story to life. We also wanted to use the immediacy of the Storyline to help the children personalize the experience of being a slave and give them an understanding of the tremendous courage and conviction that it took to fight for basic rights.

As this was a new type of topic for both of us, we took the time to sketch out a possible layout in the classroom for the story as it unfolded. We drew the back wall of the room where most of the work would be displayed; then we broke it down to see what we could put where, so that the whole display told the story as it unfolded. We knew that the careful, attractive display of the students' work would be critical in giving the story shape and focus. We also felt that this would promote ownership of the story. If we, as teachers, take the time to carefully and attractively display student work, then we are giving children the message that their work is valued, and this in turn inspires them to produce their best work. As completed work is mounted in the classroom, the sense of pride grows, and the children become more and more committed to maintaining the high standards that have been set.

Throughout this Storyline, Rebecca and I were meeting daily to see how things were going in each of our rooms, talking through what was happening, and making plans for the next episode. I couldn't have done such a demanding topic without Rebecca's support. Storyline demands close collaboration because it is such a carefully designed way of working. There are so many places where a teacher can get stuck or confused while doing a topic; it is essential to have the support of a colleague who can be there for you—listening, giving advice, and asking questions. This keeps the whole thing moving and prevents the teacher from getting frustrated and overwhelmed.

The Storyline began with a prologue, the reading of a short piece called "Africa: The Story Begins." It introduced the children to the reasons that the slave trade was started in the United States. We then read a piece together called "The Israelites Oppressed in Egypt," which served two purposes: We wanted to set the proper context for the Storyline by helping the children to see that slavery had been a fact of life throughout much of the history of the world. After reading the two pieces, we made a compare-and-contrast list. It was interesting to see the children make connections between the Israelites and the Africans. Many of them saw the connection from their church backgrounds and understood that the stories of the Bible had provided powerful metaphors for the slaves in their quest for freedom. The stage was set for the start of our story—the reading of the first two chapters of the novel that would be our road map for this Storyline topic.

I have a cheesy old electric campfire that I inherited from one of my neighbors. It is one of those things—you might remember something similar from Indian Guides or Scouting days—that you plugged in and sat around in the school gymnasium on a winter night, telling ghost stories. It gets its flame from a yellow lightbulb made to flicker with a rotating drum of swirling clear-and-red plastic skillfully hidden underneath the realistic-looking fiberglass logs, which glowed with a lifelike brilliance as long as it was plugged in! I set this up on my rug, turned out the lights, and had the children sit in a circle around it as I read. I figured that they would think this was a bit hoaky, but they loved it! From that day on, we couldn't read the story without the lights off and the campfire on! Children fought to be the ones to sit closest to the fire. The children were excited by the story, and we made a class list of predictions about what might happen. We were introduced to two of the important characters in the story and the setting of the slave quarters on a plantation. After answering the question *What do you think this story will be about?*, we began to create some of the characters and the setting of the story. Each child was given an extract to work with, a piece of the story rich in detail that they would have enough information to bring the story to life. Here is that first extract:

> Then Mammy stood. She lifted her head high and the white headrag that covered her greying hair showed soft, and a little golden in the firelight. She straightened her shoulders, almost reaching to the top of the cabin door. Her lips drew firm and her eyes pierced deep into Julilly's. In them was the sting that a bull whip makes and the hurt of a wounded possum.
>
> "We've got to pray hard, June Lilly, and if the good Lord can't help us now, we've got to believe He's going to help us soon."
>
> "Yes Mammy." Julilly felt pride in this tall, handsome woman.
>
> "There's three things I want to say to you, child." Mammy drew Julilly close again. "Pray to the good Lord. Remember to be proud that you had a strong, fine Daddy, and a Mammy that loves you."
>
> Mammy Sally paused. She pressed her mouth against Julilly's ear. "This is secret talk I'm tellin' you now. Hold it quiet in your head and never let it out your mouth. There's a place the slaves been whisperin'

around called Canada. The law don't allow no slavery there. They say you travel north and follow the North Star; when you step onto this land you are free."

Rustling footsteps outside the cabin caused Mammy's arms to stiffen. She pushed Julilly gently away and, lifting her voice, spoke crossly.

"Now, June Lilly, you crawl down on that blanket in the corner and go to sleep. Before you know it, four o'clock will be around and the morning bell will be ringin' for another day's work."

Talking for those who might be listening from the outside was always different from talking inside to those around you. Julilly knew this and smiled. She lay down on the hard floor beside the fireplace and wrapped a thin blanket around her. "Canada." She thought the name again and again in her head.

The slave trader meant some kind of trouble. But there had never been trouble on the Hensen plantation. She and Mammy Sally wouldn't be sold.

Julilly yawned and hummed a little tune, and the unsung words made her smile and forget the trouble filled day.

Massa sleep in the feather bed,
Black folk sleep on the floor;
When we get to heaven
There'll be no slave no more.

The children were given six tasks; they chose the one they wanted and worked in groups of four. Two groups were to make X-ray models of a slave cabin. A piece of cardstock folded in half was used to show both the inside and the outside of the slave cabin. Two groups were to work on making posters advertising the sale of slaves. The remaining groups created 3-D portraits of Julilly and Mammy Sally to hang in the display area. Rebecca and I had gotten some books from the library and had done some Internet searches to get together a small resource library for the kids to help them get started. It was now most important that the children create their idea of these things. The power of ownership inherent in the child's conceptual model convinced us that this is always the place to start.

As the groups finished their work, I mounted it on the back board. The slave cabins ended up being made with Popsicle sticks glued to the paper so they were freestanding. I covered a two-place table with black paper and set them up on that at the base of the back bulletin board. The slave advertisements had the left corner of the board and the portraits were put up above the board on either side. Rebecca and I put a huge arch of black butcher paper up above the board that reached to the ceiling because we wanted the night sky to be over all of the work. This would be where the children would eventually put up their models of the constellations they would create later on in the topic. The night sky was a symbol of freedom to the slaves and the drinking gourd showed the road to freedom. We wanted a strong visual reminder of this metaphor to always be in the minds of the children.

Next, we made "Underground to Canada" journals. We knew that we didn't want to make topic books at the conclusion of this Storyline; the journal would be the place where children would accumulate all of their work as the Storyline progressed. We used legal-sized paper with laminated construction-paper covers, which proved to be quite durable. The books were stapled in the middle with a long-armed stapler, and each child was given a laminated line guide so that writing on unlined paper was not a problem. The line guides were kept in the journals with a paper clip. These journals never went home; they were kept in a box in the classroom and passed out as needed. The children were given a white piece of paper and a set of pastels to design a cover and they could decide what to call their journal. These papers were glued to the blue covers before laminating. There was a lot of variety in the designs and the titles. This was a good idea because it allowed each child to establish his or her own personal statement about the story.

Figure 8–1. Close-up of the slave cabin

The first thing the children put into their books was a map of the eastern United States with nine points on it showing the route to freedom. Corresponding to the map, each child drew nine circles to record the "people they met on the way." The story is about a journey, and the children needed to see the importance of all who helped the girls reach freedom. As the story unfolded, we would update the map, writing in the distance to the next stop, labeling it, and listing all of the people that were involved in that leg of the journey. The kids who finished first made a large map to put up on the class display, which we could refer to.

The next three chapters of the book were read during this time. Julilly was separated from Mammy Sally and sold to a plantation in Mississippi. A passage of the book describing the arrival at the new Riley plantation was given out to pairs of children; they read the passage together and answered questions about it in their journals. This was designed to give the children important background information for the rest of the Storyline. By now, they were completely immersed in the story and started bringing resources from home to share with the class. Our music teacher, Nedra Schnoor, began to work on spirituals. She teaches music using a system called Orff Schulwerk, which stresses the making of music, so the children were learning to play instruments, sing the songs, and develop creative movement to go with the spirituals. During the course of the Storyline the children learned four spirituals.

A Storyline topic starts small and grows bigger, starts slow and gets faster. As the children are drawn into the story they begin to make connections in other subject areas and in other areas of their lives. As these connections are made, the Storyline is all-encompassing in the children's minds and moves quite swiftly to its conclusion. This whole process takes anywhere from four weeks to several months. Because of the richness and depth of the subject, Underground to Canada took four months.

By the time Julilly had reached the new Riley Plantation, the children began to understand why the slaves would want to escape. Julilly had become friends with Liza, another slave on the plantation, who had tried to escape. When the overseer, Sims, had caught her, he whipped her so badly that she had scars all over her back and she walked with a limp. We read the picture book *Follow the Drinking Gourd* to see how the slaves managed to get to the north and freedom. The children were astounded by their dependence on the stars to show them the way.

What do you know about the constellations? I asked the class. Armed with books on the constellations, groups of three children chose a constellation to study and made models using glow-in-the-dark stars, and gold and silver paint. They wrote a little informational piece about their constellation in their journals. The models were put up on the night sky, shining out over the classroom like beacons of hope. The children were fascinated to learn that the slaves also relied on moss, which grew mostly on the north side of trees, to point them in the right direction when the weather was cloudy and they couldn't see the stars.

Midway through the Storyline, our classes spent a week at a camp in the Oregon high desert. We wanted to let the children experience the wonder of stars in a wilderness area, away from city lights. Although this trip was originally planned as part of our science program, it fit beautifully into our Storyline. We found natural connections like this throughout the course of the topic. One evening at our campfire, Rebecca read the title story from a collection called *The People Could Fly* by Virginia Hamilton. Together, we experienced the magic of that story and the power of hope that it must have instilled in the slaves who heard it. As we walked back to our cabins that night, I pointed out the Big Dipper and showed the children how to find the North Star.

One of our children was a foster child who had been taken from his father because of sexual and physical abuse. He was a brilliant child, but deeply wounded, and this caused him to lash out and seldom stay focused. In this environment, away from the pain and suffering of the inner city, he came alive again. One day I found him totally immersed in turning over rocks to see if there were any "little ants" at home. He was busily talking to himself, making sure that if the ants were home that he put the rock right back where he found it so as not to disturb their routine. Slowly, and for the first time, he was being healed by the warm arms of Mother Earth. On that night he stayed out longer than the others, staring in wonder at the Drinking Gourd.

"You mean that's the same Big Dipper that the slaves followed to Canada?" he asked.

"Yes," I said quietly. "The very same one."

Soon we were back at school and could continue with the story. The next extract from the story dealt with the harsh realities of life in the cotton fields.

> The sun rose white and hot, burning at the nakedness of the ragged slaves. The face of Sims glistened with sweat. It dripped down from the wide brim of his hat. None of the slaves wore hats. There was no shade for their heads.
>
> Sims' anger rose with the sun. When the work slowed, he used his whip. Julilly's fear of the man turned to despair, and then to intense dislike. She had never disliked anyone as much as this fat, squint-eyed Sims. She avoided looking at him. When he came near her she worked steadily and tried to overshadow Liza, who crouched beneath her, pulling cotton from the lower branches.
>
> Once Liza said after Sims had safely passed beyond them, "That man

thinks a slave is just like a workhorse. If you acts like a workhorse you gets along just fine. If you don't—it's the cat-o-nine-tails on your back."

The work went on—picking, filling the croaker sack, emptying it into baskets, stamping it down. The small lunch and the fifteen-minute rest seemed no longer than the time it took for a mosquito to bite.

The slaves still picked when twilight came, and the red sun had slipped away to cool its fire beneath the earth. The long walk back to the slave quarters was silent, except for the shuffle of tired feet dragging through the dust.

That night it was as dark as a snake hole in the long, low cabin where Julilly and Liza lay on their heap of rags on the hard dirt floor. There wasn't a wisp of wind and the heat of the day stayed inside like a burning log.

Julilly ached with tiredness and hunger gnawed wildly at her stomach. There had been only turnips and a little side meat served for supper. The other slave girls along the floor slept heavily, but Liza was restless. Her hand reached out in the darkness and touched Julilly.

"You is a friend," the crippled girl whispered, "no one else ever picked the high cotton my poor old back won't stretch to."

Julilly felt a strong urge to protect this beaten, crippled girl, who once had tried to run away. All alone, Liza had run into the swamp—waded into the sticky water and slept with no covering until Sims tracked her down.

The key question that followed this extract was *What do you know about the slave trade?* The children, as a class, brainstormed a daily timetable in the life of a slave and contrasted that with one for Sunday, when the slaves didn't have to work in the fields. These timetables were copied into the journals.

We talked about the economics of the Golden Triangle, and the children mounted a simple line map in their journals that showed the trade routes that formed the Golden Triangle. They labeled the products that were carried from place to place. The children were outraged as they realized what was being done to thousands and thousands of people all because of greed and money. From time to time, they were writing in their journals about their thoughts and feelings about the incidents in the story as well as the historical facts of the period.

Annie Rose wrote this, "What I've Learned About Slavery So Far":

I know that families were split up and kids were sold to other masters and had to go to the fields and pick one hundred pounds of cotton a day or get whipped one hundred times with a cat of nine tails which is a whip that has rocks and glass and stones stuck inside the whip. They would crack it on your back to make you work faster.

Many of these journal entries were written as homework. We wrote the question on a piece of paper, which they would take home, and write out their ideas. The next morning they would transfer this writing into their journals. This gave them time to really contemplate and write thoughtfully, which showed in these pieces.

The next part of the story introduced the first rays of hope into an otherwise desperate situation. A man from Canada, said to be an expert on birds, had come to the plantation to gather specimens for his collection. He wanted two slaves to act as his guides. As it turned out, Massa Ross was more than just an ornithologist; he was also an abolitionist, and he had a plan to help some of the slaves escape. He called a secret meeting in the woods where he would share his plans with those slaves he thought he could trust. The next extract the children were given detailed that meeting.

> "My conviction is that slavery is such a monstrous wrong that any measure is justified to liberate as many of you as possible."
>
> Lester interrupted, "I think these folks should know, Massa Ross, that you are one of those Abolitionists that are helping to free the slaves."
>
> "That's right, Lester." Mr. Ross' eyes became merry and he laughed softly, "I've been called, 'Negro Thief', and in one town in Tennessee a sign was put up which said, '$1,200 reward for the apprehension of the Accursed Abolitionist.' That was me."
>
> His laughter eased the tension. The circle of sturdy pine trees closed around them like a sheltering arm.
>
> Mr. Ross began speaking straightforwardly. "This is a great risk you are taking to escape bondage for freedom. None of it is going to be easy. It won't even be easy when you get to Canada."
>
> He looked at each of them steadily and in turn they met his eyes with lifted heads.
>
> "It takes courage and determination and a good deal of wit." His words were measured and slow. "If you don't think you can do it, I will understand."
>
> Julilly found it strange just to look in the eyes of a white man. How was she going to speak her mind in front of one? She was glad for the night and the darkness that covered all of them.
>
> "I'm afraid, Massa Ross. But I don't want to be whipped by Massa Sims one more time. Even a horse shouldn't be whipped the way he whips us slaves. My mammy told me to meet her in Canada and I want to do this. I've got courage the same as she has."
>
> "That's so, Massa Ross," Lester added. "She helped me out of the swamp when the chain was around my ankle."

> Julilly was pleased that Lester remembered. She knew that Lester would never stay at Massa Riley's place, even if he was whipped until he nearly died. She didn't know about Adam. He was meek and gentle. He mostly liked to sing. But he had strong arms and a proud head. His skin was as black as Liza's. It faded into the night.
>
> Liza straightened her head and stood as tall as she could. "The Lord has been speakin' to me, Massa Ross," she said simply. "He says to me, 'You ain't meant to be beaten. You is a woman same as Missy Riley.' Bein' black don't make me no animal. I got eyes, and hands, and legs same as she has."
>
> Adam was the last to speak.
>
> "Until I met you, Massa Ross," he murmured in his soft easy way, "I figured white folks had slaves everywhere."

At this point the children said we needed to make more characters. Adam, Lester, Liza, and Massa Ross were added to the portraits on the wall. They were put up with Julilly, but Mammy Sally stayed on the other side of the room by herself to show that she and Julilly had been separated.

The kids thought that the portraits would look better if they were framed, and I agreed. I showed them how to make a decorative frame out of paper, then left them to decide what to do. The group working on the frames decided that they wanted to add words to them that would say something about the characters. Julilly and Liza had frames that said "Runaway," Massa Ross' frame said "Quaker Abolitionist," Lester's frame said "$2000 Reward," and Adam's frame said "Dead or Alive." Mammy Sally's frame said "Julilly's Mammy." I was impressed with the insights that these frames gave to the characters. Clearly the children had identified with these people. There was no need to teach a separate lesson on character development; they were naturally exploring the many facets of these characters because they cared about them. This depth of involvement with the literature had never happened before in a traditional novel study, and I was excited.

The next key question that we asked the children was *What is an abolitionist?* When we put up a class brainstorm list, the children were not surprised to discover that they knew very little about the abolitionists, although they were full of ideas of what they should research. Rebecca and I had put together six different study topics we wanted the children to explore. We also had a set of criteria for the final presentation of the research. This criteria was stapled to the front of a group folder, and then each group had a place to keep their notes, resources, and information. The groups were as follows:

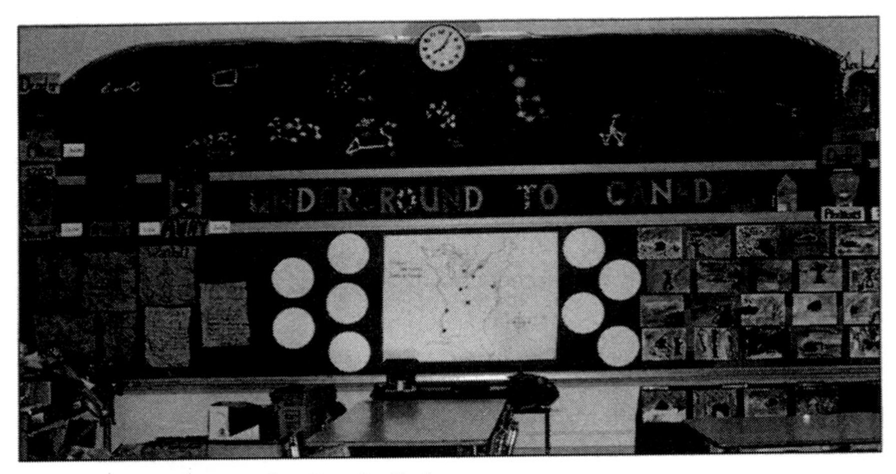

Figure 8–2. Underground to Canada display

1. Frederick Douglass
2. Abbey Kelly Foster
3. Harriet Tubman
4. Sojourner Truth
5. Slave Narratives
6. History of the Underground Railroad

We chose these particular people and subjects because we knew that there was enough information available for each of the groups to put together a presentation. We also knew that the children should be familiar with all of these people as part of their understanding of the history. We had checked out some of the best books from the library at school; I had done some World Wide Web searches and found slave narratives from the Library of Congress, abolitionist literature, and short histories of the Underground Railroad.

Here are the criteria we developed for the presentations:

1. Presentations will take no more than ten minutes.
2. You need to include direct quotes from the person\people you studied.
3. Every group member must participate.

4. Your presentation must include two or more media, i.e., songs, pictures, maps, etc.
5. The group must evaluate its members.

In my experience helping children structure research, I have found that it is important to have benchmarks that the children can hold on to. Working in a group, preparing a final presentation, and having clear, identifiable products to make up the presentation are all aids to success for fourth- and fifth-grade children. I have developed a set of five questions that I ask whenever I am doing research with children. It is a good rule of thumb to have the children address one or two of these questions, and have the teacher decide the rest. This assures that the research becomes a part of the topic, and not a long, dragged-out diversion from the story. It also gives children a template for doing research that they can apply to future projects, either for school or for their own personal knowledge.

1. Brainstorm list of questions: What do we need to know?
2. Where can we go to get answers?
3. How shall we divide up the research?
4. How will we present our research to each other?
5. What criteria will we have for our final product?

We gave the children three weeks to work on their research. In retrospect, I think it was about a week too long. The groups weren't ready after two weeks, but that had more to do with their poor use of time than that they needed more time to finish. In the end, Rebecca and I told the children that the presentations would begin on a certain date and that they would be videotaped. Both of these pieces of information had the desired effect. It is amazing how the idea of being videotaped causes children to take their work more seriously. Rebecca and I were impressed with the work our children were doing, and we thought it would be a good idea to do our presentations together so that each class could see the work the other had done. This took longer than we would have liked, but in the end, it really motivated the kids.

It was also useful to have the two classes together as the groups evaluated what they did and the rest of the children gave them feedback. The children were very positive and kind in their assessment of each other's work, even though a few of the groups admitted that they hadn't been properly prepared. Those groups spent the time they needed fixing the things that didn't meet the criteria, and then they gave their presentations again just to their own class. It was a good experience for the children to see that they could make it right and that the standards we had set were not just arbitrary, but were used to develop the best possible work from each group.

By the time the presentations were finished we had been working on them for a week. Rebecca and I could tell that we needed to get the story alive and moving again. We were losing the sense of urgency and anticipation inherent in the book. We decided to skip the next thing we had planned, because it wouldn't have helped us move the story along.

I have never done a Storyline topic where I do everything I plan. You have to be responsive to the needs of the children, the time you have to devote to the study, and the demands of your curriculum. Although the work with compasses and maps would have been worthwhile, we knew that we would be in danger of turning the Storyline into a class project fueled by the energy of the teachers rather than an exciting story playing itself out in our classrooms. It was the right decision.

We read the next extract and really spent time talking and thinking about the Underground Railroad.

> The little driver drew all of them close to him beside an open window. He placed a round glass object on the flat windowsill. A black needle quivered inside it. He showed them how it always pointed north—the same as the North Star.
>
> "I am leaving this compass with you," he explained, and he chipped it slightly with his knife a little east of north. "You must not go straight north, it is too dangerous. Follow the needle east until you come to the Cumberland Mountains near the city of Knoxville. In the mountains there are caves for shelter and Indian paths to guide you."
>
> The fugitives listened carefully. Julilly repeated the strange names over and over in her mind.
>
> The little man pushed his wide-brimmed hat back from the shadows of his face. For the first time Julilly noticed his bushy eyebrows and deep-set, kindly eyes. He talked about mountain ranges they would cross and cities they would come to. He believed they were going to get to Canada. All four of them needed this faith in their venture. They drew closer to him, more hopeful than they had been since leaving Massa Ross. The kindly man looked into the faces of each of them, as they stood quiet and expectant around him.
>
> "I just wish I could take you right to the border of Canada." There was unexpected fervor in his voice. "Slavery is a horrible evil."

He pulled a round, sturdy watch from his pocket—then checked the position of the sun in the sky. He became nervous again and spoke quickly.

"The mountains will take you into Kentucky to the city of Lexington," he said. "Here you can follow the railroad tracks by night. They lead straight north to the city of Cincinnati in Ohio and to the home of Levi Coffin. Don't forget his name. He is the 'president' of the Underground Railway."

The Underground Railway? Julilly was puzzled. Had these Abolitionist built a road under the ground all the way to Canada? She would have to remember to ask Massa Levi Coffin about this.

"God bless each of you," the little Quaker called as he ran to his wagon.

What do you think the Underground Railroad was? I asked. The children were asked to write a letter to Levi Coffin, the president of the Underground Railroad, and tell him that Lester, Adam, Liza, and Julilly were coming to his house on their way to Canada. Then they were to rewrite the letter using the code words of the Underground Railroad, so that an outsider wouldn't know what the letter was really about. We had just read a chapter in the book where the girls had spent the night in a secret room in the house of a freed slave, who, with his wife, shared many of the code words they used on the railroad. In pairs, the children wrote these letters, edited them, and did their final copies on unlined paper in pen. These were mounted side-by-side and displayed on one of the classroom walls next to the map and the portraits. I took the finished letters to the copy machine and reduced them so that each child could put a copy of both of the letters into their "Underground to Canada" journals. Here is a sample of an original and coded letter to Levi Coffin.

ORIGINAL LETTER

Dear Mr. Levi Coffin,

Two young slave girls will be on the way to your station cabin in a few days. Keep a lookout for two young slave men who were with the slave girls until they were caught. One girl is weak and has a bent back. The other is strong and tall. They have a bundle of food and a compass so don't worry.

Signed,
Massa Ross

LETTER IN CODE

Dear Mr. Levi Coffin,

I will be sending you two packages of dry goods. In a few days they will get to you. Keep a lookout for some hardware that might not get to you as scheduled. They were not put with the dry goods. One of the dry goods might be torn and ruined, the other, hopefully, will be in good shape. They will be dropped off at Jeb's station. They will have labels and a special clock for you inside the dry goods.

Sincerely,
Massa Ross

Shortly after these letters were written we read the next chapter in the book where Lester and Adam go downstream to catch some fish for dinner and are caught by the slave catchers. Julilly and Liza cower in terror in the barn where the little Quaker had hidden them and listen helplessly while the dogs bark, and Lester and Adam are chained together and taken away. We moved the portraits of Lester and Adam away from Julilly and Liza, and the story followed the two girls from this point on.

The journals now were quite full. I could see that some of the children had no idea if they were caught up with all of the work, so we took time to make a class list of everything we had done from the beginning. This became a table of contents for the journals, and as we added new assignments to the journals, I added them to the list. In hindsight, I should have done this from the beginning. Some children feel so overwhelmed when they get behind that they just stop trying. An ongoing list would have helped them to stay on top of things.

I began systematically checking each child's journal to see if he or she were caught up. This proved very helpful because the children knew exactly what they needed to have done and what they still had to finish. I was able to send some assignments home, and our resource-room teachers were able to work with some of the kids to help them get caught up. Most of the children did not see the journal as a burden: They took great pride in recording the story and sharing their thoughts. Because we had been together for two years, they saw the value of compiling a record of our Storylines. They also knew that I would not accept anything less than a completed book.

The journal, or the topic book, that we do for our Storylines follows the linear sequence of the story and makes sense to the children. They understand that it represents all the things they have learned. The table of contents list became the most referred-to chart in my classroom, and I was told promptly if I forgot to put a new assignment up on it!

We also had to update our map and our "People They Met on the

Way" circles. Both of these visuals gave the children an understanding of plot and character. They had to analyze each episode of the story and decide which people were the main characters, and they had to recall the different places that the fugitives traveled to on their way to Canada. It was a real eye-opener for the children to figure out the distances between each of the stops on the journey and to realize that these distances were traveled barefoot and in hiding.

The fifth extract described a terrible storm that the girls experienced while traveling on a mountain pass to the next stop on their journey.

> There wasn't much danger from the slave catchers on the high mountain paths at night. But even without them, this wild place was terrifying and strange for Julilly and Liza. High-pitched animal cries that they had never heard before echoed in and out of the tall black mountain peaks. Their path sometimes became "slim as the string bindin' a cotton bale," as Liza exclaimed.
>
> The girls held onto one another and once Julilly had to grab a tree limb to keep from slipping down the mountain's side. Liza fell against her, hanging onto her waist. They climbed up again on their hands and knees.
>
> "If that North Star wasn't up there steady, beckonin' to us," Julilly shuddered, "I couldn't go on."
>
> Before long, a strange, nervous wind began to blow. It skittered about–twirling up the stones along the path, then jumping into the trees and making ugly, swaying brushes of the giant pines.
>
> A cloud smashed across the moon and erased their path. It was dark now, as dark as the deep end of a cave. The air began to chill. Julilly and Liza stopped climbing and held onto the trunk of the nearest tree. The wind lashed around them like a slave owner's whip.
>
> Someplace nearby there was a long, cracking noise and then a thud. When the flashes of lightning came, Julilly and Liza could see a giant tree, torn from the earth with its raw, useless roots exposed to the storm. Thunder pounded in the sky, and the rain swept down like moving walls of water.
>
> Another flash of lightening. This time the girls saw a flat place close at hand, shielded by an overhanging rock.
>
> "Get all the tree limbs you can find, Liza, and pile them under that rock," Julilly screamed above the wind.
>
> The pile grew high. They dragged heavy limbs that could not blow away.
>
> They scraped and groveled. Their hands bled; but a small shelter did take shape, big enough for the two of them to squeeze inside. They shoved their bundles ahead of them.

> "It's dry here." Liza rubbed her hands over the ground.
>
> But their newly patched clothes dripped with water, and they chilled each time the wind blew through their makeshift hovel. There was nothing to do but take their clothes off, wring out the water from them as best they could, and hang them over branches that were still dry. They covered themselves with pine needles and bunches of dried leaves and dug deeper with the sticks into the dry earth.

What do you think it was like for Julilly and Liza in the storm? I asked the class. We had the children brainstorm a list of words that described the storm and then those that described the tranquility within the storm. We wanted the children to contrast the storm with the need for shelter and the idea that even within great danger there can be found a place of shelter and tranquility. There was a lot of anticipation because the children knew that they were going to do some artwork associated with this episode. We had a space left blank on our display wall and so they guessed that now would be the time to fill it. When I told them that we were going to be doing watercolors of the storm they cheered!

First, the kids took black paper and cut out a place of shelter in silhouette, which they glued on to their paper. Then they did a watercolor wash to depict the storm. The results were stunning. It was exciting for me to see how the children used the brainstorm list to give them ideas and then translated those ideas into their paintings. I wanted to get the paintings up soon after they were finished, and I stayed after school to do it. I put up a checkerboard of purple squares on the black background paper and then placed their paintings over that. Rebecca was inspired and used some of the painted paper the children had made earlier in the year to make clouds and raindrops and then used foil to make lightening, which became the background for the children's paintings.

Rebecca and I have grown in our understanding of the importance of display as a motivator for children. I believe that properly displaying children's work is critical because

- Good display promotes children doing their best work.
- It makes children proud of what they have accomplished.
- It allows children to revisit new learning and encourages them to share it with others.
- It helps children to see the cumulative body of their learning.
- It builds and sustains excitement through a topic.
- It furthers the principle of ownership as children value their work more when it is attractively displayed.

After the paintings were finished the kids wrote a piece for their journal telling what they tried to accomplish in their paintings. We were interested in carrying the idea of the storm as metaphor a bit further, so we had the children do a brainstorm list in which they compared the girls' normal view of blackness with their view of blackness in the storm. At first the list was all positive on the usual side and all negative on the storm side. Then one child suggested that blackness must have been comforting in the storm because the shelter they found was pitch-black, but it provided them with protection. The lists began to open up, and the children began to expand their understanding to include apparent contradictions and ambiguities.

This was a good background for writing, and the next thing the children did was to write haiku about blackness. Each child's best haiku was written on a small piece of paper and put up between the storm paintings.

Understand sadness?
Understand segregation?
Understand HUMAN?

Black, dark, unpeaceful
learn faith, learn love together
the storm, slavery

Black is not afraid
it will never be afraid
therefore I am proud

Black is beautiful
slaves run as fast as you can
black is beautiful

We were nearing the end of the story, and we decided to update the map and the "People They Met on the Way" circles. In addition, we had the children in groups of three make magnifying glasses to show an important event that happened at each place on the map. The groups were given a large circle of paper and it was up to them to choose a significant scene to represent that place on the map. These scenes would "magnify" the place and show in detail those things a magnifying glass would. The paper circle represented the lens of the glass. The final scenes were done in colored pencil, backed with colored paper, and put up around the map with a string going from the circle to the place on the map. The whole process was fascinating to watch because the children had to grapple with the main idea of each scene and try to capture that in a picture.

While we were working on these pictures we read a chapter in the book where Massa Ross meets the two girls in Cleveland, Ohio, and tells them that Adam and Lester had reached Canada and freedom, but Adam had lived only one day. He had died of blood poisoning from the wounds he got from the chains around his ankles. It was a hard chapter for me to read and even harder to see the looks on the faces of the children. They couldn't comprehend how, after all the struggle and the effort, Adam could have gotten his dream and then died. I didn't know what to say, so we sat in silence for a long time. What happened next caught me by surprise and showed me again how the children truly owned this story, just as they had owned all of the other Storylines.

After a period of almost two minutes of silence, I watched as the children one by one turned around to look at their portrait of Adam. Soon, every child was gazing up at the character on the classroom wall: our Adam. I realized that it was our Adam who had just died for my kids. As a class, we had created our vision of Underground to Canada and it belonged uniquely to our community of learners.

"Do you think we could make a pine tree and put it next to his picture because it says they buried him under a lone pine tree on the shore of Lake Erie?" one child asked.

"Yeah, and could we make a sign that says 'Rest in Peace' to put under the tree?" asked another.

We talked for awhile about chains and the incredible cruelty that they inflicted on the slaves. I have never seen a class of children understand such human suffering so deeply. The heartache and the joy that was the Underground Railway had become a part of us.

When doing a Storyline of this nature you must be very careful to end it with a feeling of hope. It is not right to let them experience such despair and then leave them there. The final extract gave us the first glimpse of freedom for Julilly and Liza. The schooner *Mayflower* carries them across Lake Erie to Canada.

> "We're gonna get to Canada, if we've got to hang onto the bottom of this boat and get pulled across Lake Erie." Julilly was angry now. What right had these men to keep chasing them right up to the border as if they were runaway dogs? She and Liza were not going to be slaves no more.
>
> It was night now. The grey fringes of daylight had slipped from the

Figure 8–3. Adam with pine tree and RIP sign

sky. Dark clouds foamed and raced above the Mayflower. Then they parted and a half moon dazzled the schooner with yellow light. The North Star shone above with radiant steadiness. A bell clanged and the boat swayed impatiently as though eager to break away from the shore.

The captain and the two large men popped out of the stairway. They heaved and puffed and ran to the entrance plank. They shook their fists in the Captain's face, but he shoved them onto the plank and waved good-bye.

The *Mayflower* turned. It swung around into the wind. The sails high above began cutting through the water.

"I feel that I'm flyin' through the sky just like those sails." Liza hugged Julilly as they both pushed a wider opening in the canvas so they could see more of the outside.

The joy that Julilly felt was so intense that there was pain around her heart.

"Liza," Julilly said finally, "Mammy Sally is watchin' that same North Star. I've got to keep myself from hopin' too much, but I'm hopin' that it's led her to freedom, too."

Liza began feeling around for the bundle of food and the flask of water. The girls ate and drank all of it. They drew the blankets close around them and watched the sails catch the rushing wind.

Without wanting to, they slept in the hollow shelter of the small lifeboat. When the captain found them later, peaceful and warm, he left them to rock through the night and be refreshed in the morning.

A crisp, bright morning came quickly with a thin, white frost powdering the deck. The air was strong with fresh fish smells. They mixed with the land smells of pine and pungent walnut bark and fertile earth still warm from summer. The waves on Lake Erie lapsed into gentle ripples. Sails were pulled in and the *Mayflower* drifted ashore.

Julilly and Liza woke with the sudden stillness of the schooner's landing. They grasped each other's hand for comfort, at once remembering the *Mayflower*, Lake Erie, and their nearness to Canada.

They pushed up the canvas on their little boat and the bright sun showered over them. The captain ran toward them, shouting with his trilling "r's" and upturned sentences.

"Ahoy!" He waved for the girls to join him. "All passengers ashore!"

He grabbed the girls by their arms and ushered them down the plank to the shoreline. He pointed to rows of tall, silent trees and the long, bleak shore.

"See those trees?" he shouted. "They grow on free soil."

Have you ever had to wait a long time for something you really wanted? I questioned the students. We wrote journal entries on this subject. We wrote about the moment when the wait was almost over. It was a rich time to write because the children had so many things to say. The story of the journey had captured all of us, and we wanted to record our thoughts and feelings.

My Thoughts on Crossing to Freedom

I think that Julilly and Liza are happy and sad. Sad because Adam died and happy that they won't be slaves anymore. And they get to see Lester! They don't have to be scared that the slave catchers are going to come and get them anymore.

I would feel excited, wonderful, delightful, happy, grateful, thankful, reflective, lovely, happy, full of joy, like a million dollars, overwhelmed, free!

What do you think a schooner looks like? was the next question. In groups of three the children did drawings of schooners. We had a few pictures to refer to, and because we had done such a wide variety of artwork throughout the topic, I was confident that the children could pick a good medium to do their drawings. They chose watercolors, oil pastels, crayons, or colored pencils. The drawings were large and looked magnificent. We made a background of blue with blue cellophane waves and iridescent glitter for foam and put the schooner pictures up high above our letters to Levi Coffin written in code. The children decided where the work would look best and helped me hang it.

The final journal entry involved writing in the first person as Julilly, Liza, Lester, or Mammy Sally, about their reunion. As it turned out, Mammy Sally had made it to St. Catherine's and was working as a cook in the hotel kitchen. She was planning to save her money to build a little house for Julilly, Liza, and herself. Here are a sampling of those entries.

JULILLY

A wide smile crept across my face. Suddenly my smile faded away. No one else was smiling. Everyone was frowning and everything was grey. But I have Mammy Sally's warmth and smile, Liza's friendship, and Lester's tenderness. When I put that all together I have love.

MAMMY SALLY

Oh Lordy, I'm so happy to be with my Julilly. I don't know what to do. I'm trying to teach her the warnings of freedom, but I guess I should just celebrate. I couldn't be happier at all than to have my Julilly back with me in freedom. Our reunion was wonderful.

LESTER

I'm so thankful to have a job and to see Liza and Julilly again. Now I know this Mammy Sally person Julilly keep talkin' 'bout. She a real nice lady ya' know. I'm so happy to be in Canada. I just feel so sorry for Adam.

The children who finished their schooners concentrated on doing the final entries in their journals. They brought them to me as they were finished, and we looked at them together to see that everything was there. It was a special time for me to spend one-on-one with each child, and to make specific comments on the writing, artwork, and design of the journal. The kids felt on top of the world when they were checked off for having completed their journal. They knew what a great accomplishment it was.

How should we celebrate Jullily and Liza's freedom? was the next, and last, question. We were near the end of the Storyline and yet we knew

Figure 8–4. Our completed freedom journals

that we needed some way of celebrating all that we had learned. We decided to do a presentation that we would invite parents to, called "Underground to Canada: A Freedom Celebration."

The presentation came together quickly. We decided to turn three of the extracts into dramatic readings, and the children tried out for the different parts. Everyone participated in the four spirituals they had learned in music. There were opportunities for singing, instrumentation, and movement. We added a section called "Thoughts about Slavery" and one called "Thoughts about Freedom" so that children could share some of the writing they had done in their Storyline journals. We compiled a rich variety of poetry, journal writing, and quotes. In spite of the usual hecticness that accompanies the end of school we worked feverishly to prepare our freedom celebration. We carved out extra rehearsal times when we could, and children memorized lines overnight. Because our timeline was so tight we quickly replaced anyone who wasn't prepared. The children were in total agreement with this because they saw how important it was to be prepared by our deadline. Invitations were written, refreshments organized, and the big day was upon us before we knew it.

It was the Thursday of the last full week of school and after an unseasonably cold, wet spring we were experiencing a glorious, warm, sunny, early summer day. It was field day at school, and the kids' minds were not on the presentation. We had our dress rehearsal in the music room and it was like pulling teeth to get them to concentrate and focus on the music and the speeches. Rebecca, Nedra, the music teacher, and I kept looking at each other and rolling our eyes. Would they really be able to pull it off in the afternoon without a rehearsal in the gym? We were also feeling the strains of the end of the year and wondering why we had waited so long to do this!

We came back to the room to get ready for the refreshments following the performance. The classroom was a mess, and I hoped that the motivation of cleaning it up for their parents would direct the kids' energies. I knew that I was having little effect! The kids' "Underground to Canada" journals were set out to share with parents, and the room was soon spotlessly clean. They cleaned up our supplies area known as the Creation Station and put a black butcher paper skirt around it to hide the junk underneath. They took down all of our brainstorm charts and trimmed the tattered edges and put them back up chronologically. They finished the final work on the magnifying glasses and straightened out all of the displays around the room. I was busy doing individual reading inventories at the time so all of this went on around me without my intervention or awareness. The final touch was a pyramid of plastic champagne glasses that would hold the sparkling cider, which were surrounded by doughnuts—a ten-year-old's idea of a celebration banquet!

Field day ended at three that afternoon; we had an hour to set up risers, musical instruments, and chairs in the gym, and to prepare the refreshments in the rooms. The kids were sucking on Popsicles, running

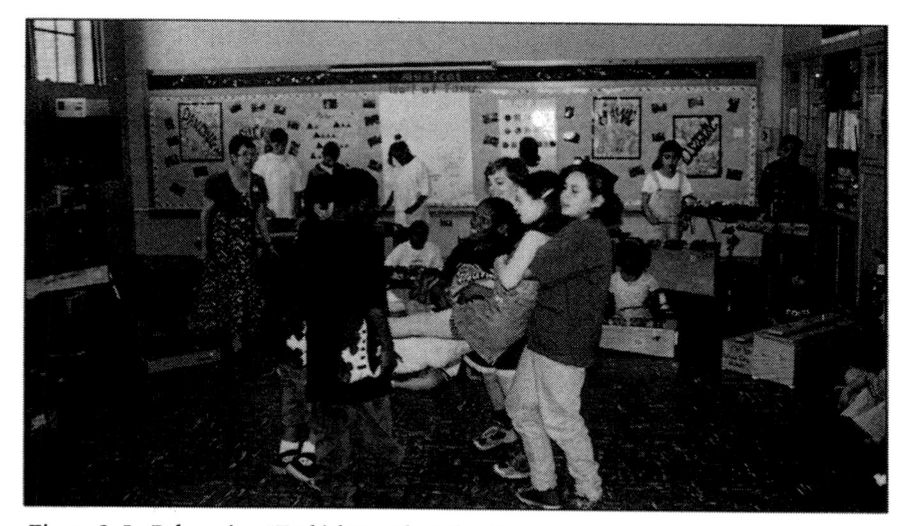

Figure 8–5. Rehearsing "Ezekiel Saw the Wheel"

around screaming, and were generally out of control. We managed to get the instruments arranged and wandered around aimlessly with our clipboards, suffering from near heatstroke trying to pull together some semblance of order before the parents arrived. I felt that we had made a mistake on attempting this at all. It was two minutes before we were scheduled to begin and three or four kids were in the restrooms changing into costumes while two others had gone home and weren't back yet! Suddenly everyone was there, and Rebecca and I were making our introductions to the parents. The children were quiet for the first time all day.

"We want to welcome you to our presentation 'Underground to Canada: A Freedom Celebration'," I said to the parents. "This represents four months of intensive study, and we are pleased to have this opportunity to share what we have learned with you. Please remember that this is not so much a performance as it is a sharing of what we have done together. Our study, which was based on a novel and had a strong historical focus, was one of the most difficult and challenging Storyline topics we have ever done. It was also the most compelling. We hope that you will catch a glimpse of some of the richness of this story and that you will sense our enthusiasm and commitment to what we have learned."

The first song in the program was "Ezekiel Saw the Wheel." The gym was silent, and the mesmerizing sound of the bass bars and the metalliphones began to rise out over the audience. The first group of children moved onto the floor to begin their movement/dance routine. Six different groups performed on each of the six verses, while the rest of the children sang the verses and played the instruments. The magic was working. Children silently moved on to the next part of the program, a dramatization of the first extract from the book. The commitment on the part of each child was complete. I had a wide smile plastered permanently across my face as I realized that the parents were having the privilege of seeing the wonder and the mystery of what these children had learned and accomplished. Rebecca and I stood on the sidelines as Nedra conducted the music from the front. It flowed so smoothly that you would have thought they had rehearsed for weeks.

I was unaware of the time passing until we were at the final song, "Wade in the Water." The children had written the musical accompaniment for this song with Nedra's help. It was the first song we taught the kids at the start of the Storyline when we were discussing the development of spirituals. We wanted to end with this song because it had become a theme for our community of learners, and the power with which the kids sang it was pure and strong.

We had a group of five African American boys who had been elected to be the "You Got To" chorus. At the end of the verses, right before the refrain was repeated, they were to shout out "You got to!" as the rest of us sang, "Wade in the water. Wade in the water, children, wade in the water. The Lord's gonna trouble the water." So often when we sang the song in class, the chorus would be too cool to really give themselves over to the task, leaning on tables and chairs, mumbling, giggling, forgetting to come in. This time even though they were each playing instruments, their shouts filled the gym. The glow of their smiles practically lifted them into the air, and I felt like I could have flown with them. It was a joyous, exuberant celebration of our work together. The rhythm of the song slowly built through the verses, and by the end we had everyone clapping, enveloped in the magic of our song.

After the song's conclusion there was a long silence, until the parents slowly began to clap. The applause continued to rise in volume and soon the parents were rising too, moved by the dedication, commitment, and passion that they had witnessed. They clapped for three full minutes, and I thought the kids would never stop smiling. Everyone helped put chairs away, take instruments back to the music room, and fold up the risers.

Parents kept coming up to me, thanking me for the presentation, and saying how impressed they were with all that the kids had learned. One parent in particular made a comment, which expresses simply why I am committed to teaching this way: "This is what school should always be like."

9 *Final Considerations*

The previous chapters have taken you through the experience of five different Storyline topics, and in the process you have seen how a Storyline unfolds in the classroom as well as the variety of forms a topic can take. I hope the first few chapters provided you with answers to some questions regarding the theory behind the method and the issues of scheduling and planning. Now that you have an idea of what a Storyline topic looks like in the classroom, I want to address still other issues, namely, junk boxes and stuff, behavior management, dealing with parents and administrators, and assessment.

Junk Boxes and Stuff

Through reading the narratives of five different Storylines you learned that the Storyline method requires a teacher to have a large supply of materials for building, creating, constructing, and mounting work. When I first started teaching this way I simply headed for the school supply closet and stocked up on the usual: tempera paint, construction paper, yarn, glue, scissors, butcher paper, crayons, felt pens, watercolors, paintbrushes, and tissue paper. I wrote a letter to parents asking for things like fabric scraps, small pieces of wood, shoe boxes, pipe cleaners, glitter, sequins, buttons, ribbon, used glue guns, or any other treasures that they might have lying around the house. At first, all I got was fabric scraps, but that was enough to get us started. I found that as the children saw a need for something we didn't have, that supply would magically appear.

One year, when I was doing a theatre Storyline, I had a group that wanted to build a life-sized stage that would extend from the bulletin board. I told them that it was fine with me, but I didn't have any pieces of cardboard large enough. If they wanted to bring in some appliance boxes from home, they could, but I didn't have any. I was hoping that would put a damper on the idea. The next day one of the fathers arrived with two huge refrigerator boxes and, to my surprise, our life-sized stage, complete with actual footlights, was born!

Keeping all of this junk orderly is an ongoing problem. I started out with plastic garbage bags, because they were free for the taking from the custodian. They soon ripped, and the contents spilled out all over my room. When the kids designated a large, six-place table as the "Creation Station," we were able to store things on and below the table. The beauty of having a spot under the table was that in times of dire need a well-placed butcher-paper skirt could cover a multitude of sins! I tried using boxes to separate supplies. Figure 9–1 shows our Creation Station in the cardboard-box phase, before it was cleaned up for our Underground to Canada Freedom Celebration. These boxes worked for awhile, but they too succumbed to the ravages of heavy use over time. Last year I purchased four large Rubbermaid tubs: one for paper, one for fabric, one for yarn and bookmaking supplies, and one for goodies like sequins, glitter, pipe cleaners, buttons, colored cellophane, gold and silver paint, tin foil, feathers, wiggly eyes, colored Popsicle sticks, and so on. These have made all the difference in the world. I assign a different child to a tub, making them responsible for seeing that everything gets back in its proper place at the end of each work session. Over time I have added five or six plastic dishpans, which hold things like yarn, hammers and nails, tape, and

Figure 9–1. The Creation Station

scrap cardboard. I inherited a low, fairly deep table from our computer lab; this makes an excellent Creation Station because I can spread everything out in a single layer. Kids can see what they want and can get it without upsetting something else. I find that the kids want to keep things neat and orderly as much as I do. They know how important it is to have the right material for the job, and they value the high standard of the projects they are able to produce with our wealth of materials.

Each year I am given a small sum of money to purchase supplies for my room, and over the years I have used this money to add to my collection of Storyline goodies. I don't think you need a lot, but interesting materials will spur children's creativity. I recently added paper, printed to look like fabric, to my goodies box, and this has encouraged all kinds of new ideas. I have a rule that no one goes into the goodies box but me. If a child wants something from the box he or she tell me what it is, what it will be used for, and how much will be needed, and then I get it for him or her. This prevents wasting materials and encourages children to make good use of the special supplies.

Behavior Management

When teaching teachers about Storyline, the questions asked most frequently are of the "what if" variety: "What if a kid doesn't buy into the Storyline?" "What if you have a kid who can't work in a group?" "What if one group finishes way before the others?" "What if the kids mess up the room and waste the materials?" Storyline is a more open way of teaching than many teachers are used to, and this can be scary at first. At the same time, it is also a much more motivating way to learn, as children want to work on the topic and often show a high level of focus and concentration that is very exciting to teachers. However, the Storyline method is not a panacea and will not solve all the discipline problems in a classroom.

I have a clear set of class rules and consequences that the children and I have developed collaboratively. Our system involves a series of warnings that I keep track of on a clipboard. During Storyline time I still use this system, just as I do when we are not doing Storyline. My role in the classroom when children are working on an extended project is that of facilitator: I go from group to group and make sure that its members are working. If I see a child who is distracting the group or not being a team player, I give him or her a warning with a clear consequence attached to it. This usually involves being removed from the group and having to work alone. I find that in most cases children who have trouble are poor listeners and are more concerned about having their ideas heard than with getting the job done with input from everyone. If the child is unable to work independently, then he or she becomes "married to my hand." Together we go around to other groups, and I ask each group if they have anything they need done. I try to come up with a specific task that the child can do to help a group. When we find such a task, I give the child the chance to complete that task, and then I come back within a few minutes to see how things are going. If the child is able to do this successfully then I allow him or her to return to the original group with a specific task for the child to do. This sequence of events almost always works. When it doesn't, I send the child to another classroom with materials to complete the task of the group alone. The next time we work on the Storyline, the child has the chance to join the group again. I find that group members are usually very willing to give the person another chance.

One of the strengths of Storyline is that it provides a compelling reason to learn, within a context that everyone cares about. This helps tremendously with children who say they are finished early: when this happens, I usually ask the group to first look at the work of the other groups and see if their own work is up to the standards set by everyone else. If the group rushed to finish and they see that their work doesn't measure up, they usually will go back on their own and improve what they have done. If they truly are finished and their work is acceptable, then I ask them what else needs to be done. Perhaps a sign needs to be made or a new board needs to be covered to accept some new work. Sometimes other groups will ask for help with their work because they are behind.

It is important to remember that just as the Storyline method is a new way of working for teachers it is also a new way of working for kids. They need to be given the time to change their thinking and the way that they do things just as teachers need that time. If I am doing a Storyline for the first time with a group of children who have never worked this way before, I have different expectations than I do for a group that has done several Storylines. I have found that over time children become much better at group work, they improve the presentation and quality of their work, and they raise their standards to a higher level with each Storyline. This is a process that takes several years.

When I visited classrooms in Scotland, I was struck by the high calibre of work I saw in the fifth- and sixth-grade classes. In one sixth-grade classroom the children had independent journals that they were allowed to work in for forty-five minutes a day. They were told that they could do anything they wanted related to their Storyline, which happened to be a topic on whaling. These journals were amazing pieces of work that included poetry, anatomical drawings, maps, research, photographs, charts, and graphs. These things were all self-generated. One group of five boys had used their recess time to construct a model of a whaling ship using cardboard and string. They had made sails out of muslin and added such details as icicles of dried glue hanging from the riggings. I listened for fifteen minutes while they explained everything they had learned. When I asked the teacher how she got such amazing work from her students, she said, without hesitation, "I benefit from all the good teaching that these children have received before they come to me. The standards for student work is so high and the children take such pride in what they do that they would be embarrassed to do anything less than what you see." In this particular school every teacher used Storyline, so the children had been working this way all along.

Last year my own class was invited to attend the concluding event of a Storyline in another classroom in the school. It was the first Storyline topic that this class had done, and my children knew that. We had done four Storylines together at this point. When we returned to our classroom the children wanted to talk about what they had seen. They were very complimentary at first and were careful to point out all of the good things they had noted. Then someone cautiously mentioned that much of the presentation had the mark of beginners. They reminisced about their first Storyline topic and how much their work had improved since then. I was impressed that these comments were not judgmental, but that the children were aware of the fact that work improves with time and practice and high standards.

I can honestly say that over time my classroom has become easier to manage. Children are more self-directed. The work is meaningful, and the children personally care about it. These qualities mean that children are doing the work because they want to, not because the teacher has told them they must.

Parents and Administrators

The Storyline method is immediately engaging for children. I have never known a group of children not to buy in completely and take off on the adventure with me. But we are not only working with the children: we also have to communicate with parents and administrators, who may be unfamiliar and therefore uncomfortable with this way of working.

Most administrators are concerned that we teach the curriculum required by the school districts in which we work. My principal wants to know that I am aware of the curriculum goals set by our district and that I can demonstrate that the children can meet those goals. I make it a point to share my Storyline topics with my principal before I start and I'll show her my goals for the study. At the conclusion of the Storyline I show her the assessment data I have collected, which indicates that they have indeed met the goals set out for them.

My principal took the Storyline class with me the summer I took it from Steve and Kathy. After seeing its power in my classroom, she was convinced. I make it a point to invite the principal to our concluding episode in the Storyline, and when possible, she also plays a part. The positive feedback she receives from parents has given her further evidence of the effectiveness of Storyline in my classroom. This fall, during our Campaign Storyline, she was the dignitary who announced the winner of our election for president and then conducted the inauguration ceremony.

My principal is my staunchest supporter, and she has encouraged others on the staff to take the Storyline training. She sees Storyline as the ideal method for integrating the curriculum and meeting the goals of the new state standards in Oregon. I feel very fortunate to have an administrator who has taken time to understand the way I teach.

Parents, on the other hand, want to know that their children are happy and engaged in school. They also want to be reassured that their children are progressing. I have found that an open-door policy is the most effective tool to communicate with parents. I encourage every parent to spend time in the classroom while we work on our Storyline topic. Actions speak louder than words: parents are usually struck by the children's commitment and passion. This, in addition to regular letters keeping parents up-to-date on our progress through the Storyline, helps parents to understand and support what we are doing.

The final presentation or grand opening is another powerful tool to inform parents about the Storyline method. Parents comment on the high degree of understanding and the sophistication of the presentations at these events. I don't have to justify what I am doing: they can see for themselves.

Last, the topic books that every parent and my principal see once a year are convincing evidence that the children in my classroom are learning the curriculum. I have watched children take an hour to walk their parents step-by-step through their topic books, explaining every last detail. The first year that I held student-led conferences I was nervous that the children wouldn't know what to say. I had scheduled three conferences each hour, and I figured that I would have a lot of dead time in-between. Most of the children used the whole hour, and my presence was rarely needed. The Storyline method is a linear way of working; the children feel very comfortable, because what they're really doing is just telling a story. The topic has a logical, linear progression and builds to a natural conclusion. This kind of focus and sense of purpose demonstrates and supports the children's deep level of understanding.

Assessment

The things I have described about Storyline may sound wonderful and exciting; but if I cannot give concrete evidence that my students have learned the curriculum, I have failed. I want to demonstrate that each child has grown in the development of his or her skills in the areas of literacy, mathematics, and research. This is why meaningful assessment is such a key piece of every Storyline topic I do. By its very nature, the Storyline method provides natural opportunities for children to demonstrate competence in all areas of the curriculum that the topic involves. The key for me is to decide which pieces of work I will use as formal assessment tools.

In the course of a year I have my children make one topic book. These books are a linear record of a topic from beginning to end. I have the children reflect back on the Storyline at the end of the study and decide what they should put in the book to record the significant events of our work together. The materials in a topic book fall into four categories: children's writing and artwork completed during the Storyline; reflective pieces of writing written for the topic book after the study; copies of class charts that were used during the study, typed and copied for each child in the class; and photographs of the frieze and important characters.

We begin the process of making a topic book by creating a table of contents that lists the items for the book in chronological order as the story unfolded. Many of the pieces are completed and filed by date in the children's working portfolios so all they have to do is get these out, mount them on black paper, and glue them into the book. Volunteers take the important class charts to the computer center and key them in so I can print a copy for each child to go into their books. Large pieces of work are folded and placed in construction-paper pockets in the book; small characters are often displayed behind a paper door or placed in a pocket. I make color photocopies of the photographs the children choose, and these are usually the last things to go in the book. All written work is done in ink on unlined paper to make it look professional.

The covers of the books are made of double-thick butcher paper, folded over a piece of shirt cardboard or oaktag for stiffness. Each book is hand-stitched by the child, using a figure eight or a Japanese binding. Most books have a black butcher-paper spine that adds to the overall strength of the book. We also give thought to the kind of endpaper we want. We have done block prints, straw painting, and marbleizing for the endpapers of various topic books.

The children also develop a criteria for evaluating the completed topic books. This often is the most powerful motivator for children to do their best work. After the criteria is developed the children have clear goals that they are working toward as they create their books. When I have determined that the children have had enough time to complete their books I set a deadline. Everyone, finished or not, knows that after the deadline there will be no more class time given to working on the topic books. It takes a lot of time, but I have each child then share his or her book with the whole class and the children rate each others books according to the criteria. It's useful to give each criteria a point, so that in the end each child gets a point score for his or her book. We also determine as a class what an acceptable passing score should be. Any child who does not get a passing score is given two weeks to make the necessary changes in the book and resubmit it for class evaluation. Over the years I have found that the following criteria work well:

1. *Contents:* The book gets a point for contents if it contains all the pieces that the class decided should be in the book.
2. *Presentation:* This point is given if the book is well put together, everything is attractively mounted and displayed, and attention is paid to neatness.
3. *Writing:* When the child shares his or her book with the class, I read one of the original pieces of writing out loud. The child gets to choose which piece should be read. A point is given if the writing represents the best of what the author can do. Because the children have many opportunities to share their writing in writers' workshops, they know each other's writing and are aware of each other's strengths.
4. *Artistic Effort:* A point is given for the visual work in the book. You do not have to be a natural artist to get this point. Many children take the time to decorate each page in the book or draw borders around their written work. Children take great pride in making their books artful and attractive.
5. *Extra:* This is a discretionary point, which I give if I feel that the child has gone over and above the requirements in any respect. I may give an extra point if a child has overcome a problem in writing or researching or if I see that the child has pushed him- or herself to a new level of competence. I am always specific about why I am giving the extra point, and I sometimes give an extra point to children who did not meet all of the other criteria. Usually the children spontaneously applaud when I give an extra point, because they recognize it as a real accomplishment for that child.

The children usually decide that a *4* is the lowest possible passing score, since all the criteria are attainable by everyone. It is a remarkable process to witness the children sharing and scoring the topic books. They are honest with themselves and with each other. When a child does not get a passing score, he or she knows precisely what they must do to raise that score. Most of the children say right up front what they still need to do if they haven't reached criteria in any area. The other children are very encouraging and careful to affirm the strengths of the book, even if one criteria is not met. After the two-week window, if the children resubmit their books and they have not reached a passing score, I arrange a parent conference to talk about ways that the family can help the child to complete the task. *Failure to attain a passing score is never an option.* This insistence on quality and high standards helps each child to challenge him or herself to continually improve. The atmosphere in the classroom is one of an encouraging learning community.

I plan to have the topic books completed by the time I do student-led conferences in the spring, and these books become the cornerstone of the conference. As the children talk their parents through the Storyline with the help of the topic book, they are sharing all the things they have learned and demonstrating all of the new skills they have acquired. Children often choose pieces from the topic book to be included in their permanent portfolio, because they represent their best work. I make sure that I build into the topic book evidence to show that the children have met all the goals I planned for the topic.

When I use a journal instead of a topic book in a Storyline, the journal becomes a powerful tool for assessment as well. Although a journal usually contains the first draft of a child's work, I will ask them to produce a final draft of certain pieces, which will then go in their assessment folders. This points out the importance of preplanning. I know ahead of time what skills and goals I am focusing on and what pieces of evidence will demonstrate competence. In a typical Storyline using a journal, I will ask the children to produce a final draft of three or four pieces of work. These pieces could be written work, drawings, maps, charts, graphs, or diagrams.

The concluding episode in any Storyline provides an ideal opportunity for meaningful assessment. At a grand opening or a final presentation, children must reflect on the important things they have learned and discovered, and they have to decide how to share these with family and friends. The Storyline provides a meaningful context for children to demonstrate what they know or what they have learned. This might take the form of a speech, a dramatization, the recitation of a poem, or the lyrics to a song. Oftentimes, the children come up with ideas for these presentations that far exceed my expectations, because they are so proud of what they have done and they want to show it off.

Because the Storyline topic provides a meaningful context to teach required curriculum, some teachers have found that at the end of a Storyline unit they can give the same test that they would when teaching more traditionally. They are often surprised to find that the children do better on the test after doing a Storyline topic because they have learned the material in a way that has made sense to them.

Where to Go from Here

If you are interested in learning more about the Scottish Storyline Method, you should take a Storyline I course. Courses are offered through a small company called Storyline Design, which Kathy Fifield started to teach this method to teachers in the United States. There are two offices: one in Oregon and one in California. The address is listed below along with the phone number and e-mail address. Storyline Design teaches several courses on the Scottish Storyline Method, and also publishes a quarterly newsletter called "The Storyline Connection." I would encourage you to call or write for more information about courses that may be offered in your area or to be put on the Storyline mailing list.

Storyline Design—Northwest and California
333 State Street #246
Lake Oswego, Oregon 97034
Phone/Fax: (503) 691-0553
E-mail: storylin@teleport.com

Life is short and we do not have much time
to gladden the hearts of those who travel
the way with us. So be swift to love; make
haste to be kind.

Henri Frederic Amiel
Journal, 16 December 1868

The author and publisher wish to thank those who have generously given permission to reprint borrowed material:

Excerpts from *Underground to Canada* by Barbara Smucker. Copyright © Clarke, Irwin & Company Limited. Reprinted by permission of Penguin Books Canada Limited.

Excerpts from *Runaway to Freedom: A Story of the Underground Railway* by Barbara Smucker. Text copyright © 1977 by Clarke, Irwin & Company Limited. Reprinted by permission of HarperCollins Publishers.